The Only Magic We Know

The Only Magic We Know

Selected Modjaji Poems

2004 to 2020

Edited by Marike Beyers

Copyright for this edition Modjaji Books 2020
www.modjajibooks.co.za

ISBN 978-1-928215-88-2 (Print)
ISBN 978-1-928215-89-9 (ePub)

Cover artwork and lettering by Jesse Breytenbach
Book and cover design by Monique Cleghorn

All poems previously published by Modjaji Books.

CONTENTS

We have lived from birth in this fist of rock / And ocean

To open up words, / unfold them to paper

INTRODUCTION

Colleen Higgs (publisher, poet): *The Only Magic We Know* is a celebration of Modjaji Books as an independent feminist publisher of women's poetry. The poems have been selected from the forty-six collections of poetry published by Modjaji since 2004.

Joan Metelerkamp (poet): In a crucial way Modjaji has created the poets in this anthology simply by publishing them in the first place. Poetry by definition needs to be out in the world. Many of the volumes of poems Modjaji has published were 'debut' volumes, and then sometimes second volumes (an even harder thing for a poet to accomplish if she has no sense of where her poems might go). In my own case, other publishers were not interested enough in my work to take the risk that poetry publishing always is, although I already had six books published. And I don't think it was just inflated ego that kept me going – it was the sense that there may be one or two, or some, people out there who might feel drawn to or by the poems which felt necessary to write.

Colleen Higgs: As yet these voices from Modjaji do not, cannot, represent all, or even many, South African women. Modjaji is proud to have published poetry in various languages in parallel text and as independent publications. Although some of these are included in this anthology, most of the poems are in English. Women's voices, and particularly black women's voices, are still marginalised, although this is changing. Since the beginning Modjaji Books has addressed this inequality by publishing books that are true to the spirit of Modjaji, the rain queen: a powerful female force for good, new life and regeneration. The work of making a common literary culture in our country, with poetry as its beating heart, is still a work in progress; a thousand tentative tendrils, feelers, growths of the new and extraordinary. The work of publishing new voices in poetry in South Africa is mostly done by small publishers.

Marike Beyers (editor, poet): As editor, I've been reading, selecting, sounding these poems. Now their echoes live inside me. Holding these poems in my mind and remembering them in conversation with each other has been complex and challenging. Most of the poems I've encountered as they came out over the years. Recalled and renewed – these poems speak to me. I made lists. I made notes. I added keywords. I worried about "boxing". How could I balance poems that seemed to represent the voice and style of an individual collection with poems in conversation with each other? I arranged them this way. Another way. Read them again. There were whispers, shouts, some elbowing. Looked at the lists again, but now I couldn't hear anymore. You're just one person reading, even your reading changes… You must choose! Compiler, putter-together, chanter, chimer…

The anthology puts poems in conversation with each other. I hope readers will find the poems, their echoes, their to-and-fro and their in-between spaces as engaging as I found my immersion in these writings. The anthology is presented in four main sections, each followed by a longer work or 'series of poems' that works as a unit. Poems in the first section are mainly about selfhood and the darker difficult stepping towards others. The second follows a biographical mode – life experiences, the personal woven together with what is larger. Then follow poems on being in and from this world and time. Closing the anthology are poems on writing, the only magic we know.

I hope these poems can be for you, as for me, both familiar and strange in relationship with each other. I think of writing as a space where one can be that voice and hear that voice that has no place elsewhere. As such I wish to thank Modjaji Books for making so much of this possible and Joan Metelerkamp for her deep reading, which is a listening and continual pulling at and against the threads of belonging and words and self. And of course, the poets, for doing the minding, holding, scolding, warning, healing, making, being, work of writing. Also thank you to Amazwi South African Museum of Literature for time and resources to work on this anthology.

APRIL 2020

...when I set off
in my best body

The white room
by Phillippa Yaa de Villiers

We are from far
so far we don't even remember
when we were summoned
by some
internal message, or maybe
an invitation in the post –
and when I set off in my best body
someone else's name was on the envelope –
I was too far gone
already held in blue rubber hands
already covered in blood
already with a whole lot of people
to take care of.

The effort of living in skin
gasping and panting
hemmed in to a white cube,
burst out again, and again and again –
at six, at twenty, at thirty-four, at forty-two
each time insisting my body in,
or out, or elsewhere
from that w h i t e   room

7 dinge wat djy nie van my sal wiet'ie
by Shirmoney Rhode

1. Toe ek klein was, het ek altyd gedink 'n hond en 'n kat is man en vrou. Hoekom annes sou hulle soe baie fight?
2. Ôs het eendag touch rugby gespeel buite in'ie pad. Toe val ek. Daai was nie soe badtie – die feit dat ek in 'n bol kak geval het was.
3. Ek het eendag 'n pysie op my regte bien gekry. Die pysie was vrek seer en goud geel. Slim kind wat ek was, het ek dit uitgedruk en later homemade remedies uitgedink wat dit bieter sou maak. Sout en asyn, tamatiesous en suurlemoensap, sunlight siep en sout, selotape en sterksalf. Toe niks mee' werk'ie, was'it die kliniek, swartsalf, 'n goeie pakslae en ouma-liefde wat nou nog die lielikke nok op my regte bien bietjie bieter maak.
4. Ek droem van niks behalwe as ek dagdroem. Ma' as ek droem, dan skrik ek altyd wakker sonder dat ek wiet wat dit was wat ek gedroem het.
5. As 'n kind kon ek nooit rêrag goed Engels vi'staan nie. Dis hoekom ek eendag met 'n karrentjie aan gestap gekom het toe daa vi' my gevra was om "the broom" te bring. Broom-broom.
6. Ek het nooit vi'staan hoekom my ma altyd gelag het as ek sê: "Mammie, breakfast betieken 'n-vis-wat-brêk né."
7. As ek een dag met iemand sou kon spend, sou dit most likely my ouma wies. Al issit oek net om ha' hande te sit en dophou wat my tot mens gemaak het.

Child in a photograph
by Arja Salafranca

She is not pretty,
this child in a black costume
showing her slight belly,
her fingers splayed wide
against her hips.
Her face is a little dog-like –
too determined, too thin,
her face just a bit too grim
for her age.
The eyes are mean.
I don't like you, little girl,
for your adult-like stance,
your stooped shoulders, your scowl.
I don't like you: you could be cruel.
You are not what I ever was.

I leave you with your future stretched
out before you.
You'll make it,
I know.

Walking the lioness
by Robin Winckel-Mellish

I'm a lioness slouching
down the *Hooftstraat*
on a diamond-studded leash.

Man-eater, alter ego, alley cat,
I'm spooked by a naked gaze,
those fur-draped shoulder blades.

I'm having a hard time keeping up,
feeling my cat breath taut –
shivering inside my skin

I'll make the break,
follow a bush-scent back
into wilderness. Loose now

on the run, I'll sink teeth
into knucklebone, spill
sapphires from my mouth.

Strange fruit
by Helen Moffett

No one knows how to unpeel me.
Some days, brilliantly coloured,
highly polished, I offer
no grip for fingers.
Some days, I'm scarred and scaled,
leathery like a litchi
no suggestion of sweet pulp.
But if you can find
my invisible fault-line
and crack me open,
I am juicy inside.

Falling
    by Crystal Warren

Because I always
end up falling
I watch my feet.

I walk carefully,
wear sensible shoes.
I never run.

Because I always
end up falling
I watch my heart.

I try not to care,
to tread lightly.
I never dance.

All the things I don't know how to do
by Kerry Hammerton

Haggle at the fish market,
lean into a dying sea
smell to claim a few pennies.
Rollerblade. Run with the bulls.
Swim with the current. Stay cool
in the summer. Hold my breath.
Warm this silence between us.

flying off the handle
by Colleen Higgs

I'm tethered very lightly, if at all
a horse who only thinks she's tied,
but every time she starts or gets a fright,
she finds in fact she is no longer near the handle   at all.

I'm easily startled, flustered, worried or disturbed
not manageable even to myself,
like a dog who is not quite tame,
I snarl, lose my patience,
sometimes I feel I could even slap strangers,
for no apparent reason.

For a Change
   by Annette Snyckers

My anger is too much a lady
she does not shout
she sits in the corner and sulks.
I want to shake her, drag her out,
bring her into the light.

I want her to pummel her fists
on the table, make a noise,
I want her to wear lipstick
the colour of ripe plums
and dark roses
I want her to wear heels
and stamp her feet
I want her to be
a bitch –

but she will not oblige.

Skin matters
by Khadija Tracey Heeger

I am captive in a mish-mesh of skin
tightened
held together by the infirmities of skin intellect,
skin wit, skin talk, skin designation, skin fragmentation
skin degeneration.
I am bound in the hue that makes you carve for me
a personality, a mind, a heart, a disposition
borne out of skin matters
skin deep.

My mouth explodes into justification, explanation, expletives
to remedy my taxonomy.
I cannot speak,
my voice remains stuck
still choking on that designation, classification,
still finding as I sift through the debris more and more
and more of me
sore and so angry,
so much more of me to free
from skin tyranny.

I have swallowed my words, swallowed my heart,
swallowed my hunger.
I have swallowed my tongue and my blood and my love
to make you safe in your autonomy.
I am captive in the mish-mesh of your mind
sweating through the walls of your fear.
I will not live

here.

The dance of the mustang
    by Tariro Ndoro

but are you tired of apologizing
for being all the lines that tether you?
for occupying all the geographies that can't hold you?

remember this:
there are different ways to say a thing:
with hands, with faces, with song
I spoke with a foreign man once
I did it with my eyes
I said the word   and
Let it hover

they'll tether your tongue like they tether the geldings,
but you remain
                unbroken mustang

see how other mustangs move?
they gallop
see how they gallop?
they run
and how do mustangs run?

    With the wind.

Polite conversations

by Phillippa Yaa de Villiers

Is that your grandson, Bungy?

That colour looks so good on you with your skin

I wish I could tan as well as you

I always wished that I had curly hair

Such sensuous lips

Is that your son's girlfriend?

It really doesn't matter to me what colour you are

I am not a racist but

We blacks are not like that

While I was sleeping a forest of words grew up in my room. Fleshy stems forced through the carpet, succulents snaked up the walls and when I opened my eyes I could no longer see the door; the words took up all the air they theytheytheytheyhardened to trunks and divided themselves into leaves that became my bed and my pillow and the orange blanket that kept me warm, I could hardly see a thing never mind breathingand it was hot and stuffy and I don't know who left a panga under my pillow but next thing I was outside with a nice pile of dead wood to start a fire with.

Mermaid song

by Haidee Kotze

It's a different element: turbid, electric, saline.
You have to prove your fins
before we can let you in.

A toe to the water is not an option;
there is only full immersion,
scraping away the scales until you're just
the pulse of raw meat baptised in brine.

It's a red tide, a lick of phototactic tongue ebbing,
or a mermaid disappearing into her gills,
depending.

This place aches and aches and aches its fluorescent beat.
You have to prove your fins
before we can let you in.

Wanting
　　by Megan Hall

Wanting's a powerful word.
I don't want to be left wanting,
want to be unafraid enough to want.

Wanting puts your heart out on a string,
trawling for the thing that's wanting you.
There's no hook, except maybe forever.

Seahorse

by Sarah Frost

Once,
I curled like a seahorse
on a whispering floor;
clear careful script
filling a secret book –

Time, a numb wave
surged over me. Twenty-two
times I nearly drowned;
found myself
floating.

myth of myself
    by Christine Coates

A man took me away –
I tried to cling
but a fish sucked my skin and opened me
to a decade of convulsions –
I climbed in and out of Chinese boxes,
met a woman with fire eyes –
she gave me a key, a way out,
although she was lost herself.
Every step of the way was a continental shift –
leaving my mother, the myth of myself,
that perhaps I could be happy
under the influence of men.
But then I burst into the wilderness –
hiked across stony paths, slept under stars,
I spent weekends in heather, on high cliffs.
The path took me close to the sea –
there I found a sand dollar,
perhaps it was the currency of love –
but I could buy only a skeleton.
The years washed away – I thought I was happy –
that I'd saved the sky
under my tent's blue canopy.

"Flexi non frangi"
by Joan Metelerkamp

for us, like any other fugitive
it is today in which we live

Even then, even in the end

you'll never know
you've got to   the end

disappearing like an old man looking up
from the bloody offal of his coughed up lungs:
"are you still here?"

Once
there was
the long time of now
                    and then

it comes to you as sudden as the swarm itself
sudden swarm through every crevice into the house with
the berg wind
hot in the middle of winter or just-spring
the cloud of bees detonating
against the panes

season of boomslangs and puffadders –

don't ask why
this should come to you –
in *perfectly useless concentration* widening
the vision of happiness, freedom, freeing
as the purpose and end – telos –
come like the advent of a child longed for
to pour all your love for

bees   breaking   free –
with the scent of tarconanthus'
camphor,
bitter buchu, sweet of psorolea,
trace of salt wind dropped to breeze off the sea –

free from –
but what to –

not the old freedom of the comrades, comrade,
not any freedom to fight for
no more
"if you're not for us you're against us!"

arising like the sound of bees
like the coming of a poem
the smell of bees
like sweaty socks,
under the floorboards, honey, honey,
wax sweating in the planks in the walls, in the walls

the queen
at her regeneration
workers searching
to keep her
making their way
in through the cracks –

Rasta boy-man on the apex of the roof
like an Indian god, his straight back strong,
limbs wheeling free,
stings, thick smoke, smoking out, tar
messy down the roof sheets where internal walls are –

where did the swarm swarm
to become itself
a vast nest, shelter, sheltering
in the wild pear (dombeya) – *honey bees, come build*

where no one believed
freedom, spirit, scraped out
like so much blighted ovum, old moulded beeswax.

The house burnt now like the ground
to the ground and now
only the chimney like in the plantation, the forest, there
chimneys, foundations, sometimes, still, concrete floors,

(old ones
gone to the city,
trekked to another country)

the place, the whole
hill abandoned.

End: as in purpose: beginning
to see again
don't throw the tender inception out
with the waters of doubt –

end as in always
beginning, learning again to free
not into Freedom but freer than before
not every day but every day
learning to not restrict

"one muscle one body"

bending not breaking bending
from the top of the femur allowing
the spine its length, strength –

remember the old man, at home,
before his last fall his last
"do you think I'll never walk again",
down in the valley, as if it were a decree,

"you are free my daughter", and again,
as if in benign benison, "free" –
and carved in plain wood on the stoep,
plain for all to see, crest of the family
"flexi non frangi" –

all burnt, all gone, all up in flames –

immigrant,
fugitive, refugee
old, old story
old as the words

you have come to
old as silence you can't hear yourself think through –

amongst these ashes, now, this foreign
birdsong, these gentle strangers,
this old stone.

A series of seven poems by Kerry Hammerton

These poems were influenced by Rafael Alberti's *Concerning the Angels*. Not the specific angels but the idea of writing about angels that are not angelic but from a place of despair.

'And then the angels revealed themselves to me... as irresistible forces of the spirit, malleable to the most turbid and secret states of my nature. I unleashed them in bands, as blind reincarnations of all the cruelty, desolation, agony, terror and occasional good that was within me and closed in on me.'

– Rafael Alberti *Concerning the Angels* (1928)

The Horse Angel

of shod hoof and trotting gait
of long foreleg muscles
arrives to teach me

to stand-still
to bind with the herd

I take too long
hold on too tight

she stands on my feet
pulls in another direction

until she is herself
again cantering into
her own flight

The Sleepless Angel

My bedroom is stained
with the bitter smoke
from his cigarette.

I try and wait him out,
but he's done this before,
hunkered down

wings folded carefully.
When I am half-asleep
he will drip blood

from the ceiling; whisper
into my ears; trail feathers
across my face.

In this half-dream moment
I can smell the fearful
sweat of him,

his nicotined fingers,
the oily grime
under his nails.

The Carrion Angel

Rusted sword,
knotted hair,
blood-soaked feathers.

He smells like the end
of the world: sulphur
and festering sores.

He doesn't remember heaven
or the fall or why
other angels shun him.

He longs to be bloodied
teeth tearing through
dead and decaying flesh.

His ears are tuned to
the whimpers and dying
cries of badger, fox,

muskrat, owl – the snap
of rodent traps.

The Dream Angels

They wait for a blackened moon
then sidle in –
infecting dreams with love

and lust, and flight.
I say prayers
but they come back

grimfaced, sharpening
halberds and swords
on stolen grindstones.

Their muddy boots mar
the kitchen floor; their bloodgutted kill
stinks in pots on the stove.

To keep me honeyed
they chant mellifluously
as if they were still in heaven.

The Dark Angel

He wants to be an angel
of snowless mountains or
the east winds

but his blackness shimmers.
Bowstring pulled taut
he always aims to kill.

Coldheart. Inward.
In him
accord is impossible.

Requiem

the crow of my mind
spreads sheeny black wings

beak tears through
the marrow of my spine

tongue throttled I
caw-caw

I am going mad again
light candles

let the incense smoulder
sing the mass;

remember to burn
my bones and flesh.

The Death Angel

The city mutes itself around me
sound by sound: jackhammers,
hooting cars, the shout of flower-sellers

until his breathing
is the only thing I hear.
His shadow has become

my shadow.
When I look at the night sky
I can't see the moon

only a black void
drifting
between the stars.

My eyes die of hunger /
as I make up my life

Three poems by Katleho Kano Shoro

Love Poem to Papa I

I used to speak of your existence
in whispers
because in my circle of blackness
fatherly presence is deafening enough
without calling your virtues
by name.

Love Poem to Papa II

Mokwena,
letsatsi le le leng
ke tla ho roka.

Daughter notes

Jazz and soul soothe me and make me feel grown.
I think this means you soothe my soul and jazz up my growth.
I think I mean you are music.

Home Times

by Christine Coates

The car's headlights cutting like a butcher's knife
into the yellow fat of meat
shiny and wet in the middle.
The flanks of beef and kudu hanging in the garage
waiting for my father to make biltong.
And guns – the gleaming metal, the sound of the bolt being
pulled back,
the smell of the oil, the softness of the cloth to buff it,
guns used for clay pigeons, or the pellet guns
we aimed at bottles on a wall.

It is 1965 and I am in the back of a car driving along a dusty road
in the bushveld. My father is behind the wheel, my arms around
his neck,
the canvas bag hanging from the front of his car as it speeds
along,
hot dry days just to drink that cold water
and dark nights, the headlights searching for a signpost, or to stop
for a rest
to drink hot tea from a flask, to dip rusks,
watch birds through his binoculars, the brown leather case they
come in,
the smell of it, his Leica and its lens that concertinas out,
the taste of leather, the feel of it against my skin,
the fur of jackals sewn together in rows, tails dangling;
it was his kaross, my fingers where the eyes and ears had been.

The oily smell of the bush in the evening – I thought it was castor oil,
but it was the potato bush – when the sun is setting,
driving into the dark with a spotlight searching for bright eyes –
impala or the eyes of bush-babies jumping in the trees.
Campfires and log fires, him standing there
drinking beer from a bottle,
seeing him through the smoke,
the smell of Peter Stuyvesant,
the red glow of the tip through the night.

a memory of my parents, circa 1977
   by Colleen Higgs

He's sitting at the kitchen table
his glass of cane and coke on the formica
his voice thick and dark with anger
my fifteen-year-old voice raised like an arm
shielding my body from the blows of his word

She's at the table too, but it's afternoon
she's drinking tea, smoking cigarettes
her children crowd her in the kitchen
she's counting on something

more
than this

The great learning
by Sindiwe Magona

The silence of absence
Is a great teacher
I should know, for
I learned a lot from Tata,
Who was never there.

Married by law and
Before the eyes of God
White man's law dictated
Three weeks out of a year
Enough time to spend with family.

All through his working life
Condemned to Single Men's
Barracks; bug-infested quarters;
His hands all that was desired.
Brainless brawn, to hew and till.

Tata, your absence, a heavy silence
I grew up without solace
Fatherless, without role model
To knit my wits to manhood
No steps to follow, no man to shadow.

I am what I am through no fault
Of yours. I am what I am for

History deemed it. Your absence,
The silence, taught me only too
Well. I am what I am. Yes, I am!

Clipped / Geknip by Annette Snyckers

Clipped

On those days
I ran about the garden
like a wild foal,
my father was convinced
that little devils nested
in my mane.

White sheet draped
over small shoulders,
I was made to sit
so he could snip
to exorcise the sprites
who whispered in my ears.

I emerged bobbed,
cut straight,
in step.

Geknip

Op daardie dae
wat ek deur die tuin gehol het
soos 'n wilde vul,
was my pa oortuig
dat klein duiwels
nesgemaak het in my maanhare.

Wit laken gedrapeer
oor klein skouertjies,
is ek sitgemaak
dat hy kon snipper
om die geeste te besweer
wat in my ore gefluister het.

Ek het kortgeknip daar uitgekom,
reguit gesny,
in pas.

Sticks and stones

by Beverly Rycroft

My father is stuck now in this wooden frame and cannot argue
any more. Once upon a time, the camera breathed the same air
as him and the shutter fell. That is the only connection. But
his words escaped. He breathed on them and they pulled his
breath in and sat up. They grew feet and walked. Then they
marched. Across our generation they trekked, indefatigable:
*What the bloody hell are you doing? You are killing me. Not like
that, stupid bastard.* Some set to chopping down trees and setting
up camp. They built cabins to house them forever in the territory
of our skinny minds. Others, instead of legs, sent out shoots,
green-tipped, to curl in at the nursery windows of the babies
we eventually brought before him. *For God's sake man,* was very
popular, and, in time, *Jesus Christ what have you done to my car?*
Yet others formed armies and marched on over the battlefields of
our scarred hills. *I am ashamed to call you son. You are nothing like
the daughter I wanted. No man will ever marry you.*
Some, weary of doing the same old thing, eventually retired in
the hollows of our creaking brains, where apartments were still
waiting to be filled. They settled there forever.
Those that stayed the course, grew softer, and overweight. They
broke ranks. Their hair spun out long and white, in clumps or
not at all. They forgot to shave. Bristles glinted like shattered
ice on their pliable jaws. Instead of leaping and marching, they
began to glide, then float. Wind-light, they submitted eventually
to capture. Finally they posted fragile, white postcards home:
Forgive me.
I love you.
I was always so
proud of you.

Caliban

   by Colleen Crawford Cousins

Be not afeard. The isle is full of noises
My mother speaks in a hurt voice
Tossing her head   complaining I do not love her
I prefer horses   their godlike smell
And the tiny men we keep under the bed
My sister and I   at night we take them out
Barry Ding Five and Tex   and ride the range with our homunculi
Later we marry badly mothered men   in agreement however
With patricide, matricide   revolution etc
When I meet the real deal   the torturers
I see how well my mother tilled my soil   prepared my ground

intentions
    by Colleen Higgs

My eyes die of hunger
as I make up my life
look for forgiveness, dream onward

my face is sour, her face is hungry
for a cup of tea, for enlightenment
I'd choke her, make a stew of her carcass if I could

she has no name, she hurts all over
her teeth bleed, her memory hurts like logic
her life hurts like liquor, like broken dinner plates

I vow to do it better
not to hesitate to bring a child downstream
like gold floating in
a bowl or
a cup

Unfolding

by Jenna Mervis

After reading 'Portrait of Love' by Njabulo S. Ndebele

There is my husband-to-be,
my fiancé, bent
over the garden tap
with deliberate hands
barefoot, sweating in
the midday glare
with shadow dog beside him
that thrusts a wet nose
into his neck. There!
See that almost-husband of mine
and his capable fingers
his calculating mind
and Wednesday's re-growth
coarse against my skin
this morning before coffee
when he took my hand
passed it over his face
to kiss my palm
and murmur his desire.

There! There he is, my betrothed.
I watch from the window seat,
piled with crumpled linen
ready to be folded
and shelved
and see our life
beyond this frame,
unfold the rolling years
to that familiar point
where this pubescent union
of ours is forgotten,
this merging of two children,
led by the nose into adulthood.

There he is,
my darling promised,
becoming man
as I become woman,
unfolding into him.

Ceremonial
by Joan Metelerkamp

Was it all really only metaphorical, ritual
like nuptial candles, vows, flowers,
lilies of the field, families,
this, that, his, hers, ours, theirs, ours, our
brothers, brothers-in-law, sisters daughters sons friends
garden paths lights speakers flowers fields
tea tents drinks chairs tables cloths flowers
soup chicken cake cheese fires
suits ties skirts scarves shoes floors;

through the mud in the rain lavatories dragged on a trailer,
the mammoth generator –

when you look back you will see
everything moved itself dance-like
        effortlessly.

Ceremony
  by Robin Winckel-Mellish

The bride has arrived to welcome guests, finely
packaged in crimson silk, tiny feet, cinnabar lips.

The mother of the bride takes the daughter's hand,
a crushed lucky envelope, presses it into mine, gives her

tells her be obedient. Are not ourselves most
precious of gifts, marriages measured

in delicate balance, as warm water poured
over tea. Chrysanthemum, lily, rose,

the rhythmic stirring of leaves, signifying
the three nods of the Phoenix.

Look at the tea in appreciation
she says, before you taste.

I have received the gift of the mother-in-law.
In the cup of glass, green leaves sink

waves of water release fragrance.

marriage

by Colleen Higgs

The birds have all gone, the river is fuller
the days are shorter, and the rain is coming.
My life will end. I've seen it now, I've seen the face of death.

They came and wheeled your mother away
on a metal trolley. Instead of mohair or cashmere, they
covered your mother with a rough, grey blanket.

I can't know what you know, how you really feel
I can only surmise from how I see you spend your days
and what you come up with, what you have to show for it all after all

I'm here, not exactly waiting. I'm distracted,
busy, reading, preoccupied, thinking, dreaming.
But if you wanted to say something more to me
than paint colour, OSB, plywood, pergola, mast, tiller
screen, decking, boat, weather, wind, supper, diesel prices
I would listen.

Except, this is the way you talk to me of what is in your heart.
My own heart is thickened, hardened against your anguish.
There are gashes in our understandings
I can't know what you know.

(the last two lines come from a poem by Adrienne Rich)

Four Voices of Marriage

by Christine Coates

Paper:
the voice of blue
things not spoken.
I lost something
long ago in the desert.
For forty years
it lay hidden,
a diamond in the dust.
A flash flood carried it far.

China:
the voice of union,
here the darkness is
broken by trees.
I know the secret,
see it in a stranger's eyes
watch it in the reflection of shop windows.

Silver:
the voice of frozen lakes.
I'm trapped in ice,
the memory of sun seeps
from my heart.
A fossil recalls
a dream I once had.
I used to believe in fairies.

Ruby:
is the colour of blood
bloodlines,
the lines of connection
umbilical cords,
your body parts and mine
birth, our children
our lives

In the Beginning
by Azila Talit Reisenberger

*"And God said let us make human in our image, after our
likeness...and God saw that it was good. And it was evening and
it was morning the sixth day. Thus He finished... His work
and... He rested".* (GENESIS I:26-2:2).

Alert and ready she lay
listening
to life created inside her
out of no graspable form and void.
A new world.
                And she saw that it was good.

In her own image, after her own likeness
she created a new hope.
                And she saw that it was good.

And it was evening and it was morning
And it is

The work of pregnancy
by Colleen Crawford Cousins

Look steadily at the darkness at the pupil's centre.
The iris closes like a shutter
on the tiny germ of death.
Your body was never your own.
Wilderness has entered your life
the cry of the bush baby in the night.

Moonlight pours its cold milk on your hands.
Alone, you're shuffling your deck of cards.
You choose one, turn it over: the three of hearts
lies on the table near the wedding tree.
You are not yourself. Bone, feathers, desperate flight –
accept the death you thought belonged to others.

Lie down, you must be horizontal.
Tie your hands, your feet, your long red hair
Braid them with fine thread to grass and stone.
An insect has his road upon your arm.
Gaze back into the compound eye.
There is nothing to be done.

17th April, 10h03
by Malika Ndlovu

Of all the tormenting pictures in my head, the image of
your body, your blood draining from your limbs, your face,
collecting in your cavities, still brings me to my knees.
Blood, rose-red peeping from your lips, ears, nose, umbilical
cord, from between your legs. I am stained with this imprint
of your physicality. Blood curdling cries race through me, a
sound stream of desperation. I ache for a tangible trace of
you.

Blanket
  by Sarah Frost

Her body still heavy
from being home to a baby for nine months
holds her feelings like a basket,
full of knitting.

From these skeins of wool,
some dark with grief for independence lost,
some blood-bright with remembered pain,
many glowing with joy

she makes a tangled throw
rough at the corners.

Later, she uses it to cover the child
sleeping in the centre of the marriage bed,
as his father, intimate, unknown, edges into her from behind,
awkward, displaced.

Living in a shoe
    by Beverly Rycroft

See saw marjory daw
out you all slid and needed feeding.

The nurses showed me how.

My nipple, your mouth.
That was the start of it.
There were rules, but I couldn't follow.
Not my language.

To me, every bird
was a witch in disguise,
every rat a coach driver.
In each white corridor
signs spun laughing

            Forty miles to London
            This way first
            Follow me
            Drink this.

Reading them
I turned to stone.

Nights blazed.
I puzzled at your cries,
crazy with the quest.
A million sounds, a million shapes
to match them to until

finally
defeated
I turned to the only magic I knew,

the shapeless, angry
loving you.

Every man
　　by Dawn Garisch

Every man is possible.
Possibly a door leading to a secret garden.
Every man has a handle, hidden.
Men are locked, even to themselves.
Mysteriously, the key has vanished.

I crouch down, put my pupil to the keyhole.
The open door of me bangs impatiently
in the wind. We're lost, on all fours,
searching, banging heads.

We imagine we are looking for the same thing.

I find something green, shaped
like a keyhole. A keyhole is not
complete without a key. As a woman,
I cannot insert myself.

I imagine the garden perfect, doused
in light. It grows and lives without me, impossibly perfect
without me.

Earth Shades in Morning
by Robin Winckel-Mellish

I'm thinking about how
the other people
(Bushmen to be precise)
live off necessity
and how maidens
(and even married women)
lift their skirts and run away,
how women court men
and men court women,
how they sit together
with tangled legs.

Everything is clear
this early morning:
the landscape, burnt bark,
dried river beds
as cracked capillaries,
a cinnamon rust in the sky.
I'm dressed in shades
of tortoiseshell and oxblood,
the ashen taste of smoke
on my tongue.

A question of time
   by Makhosazana Xaba

I see you squirm,
kick and run.
I hear you whisper,
shout and scream.

I watch you fold neatly into a ball
and roll away
only to hit against rocks
that roll you back
with the same force and speed.

So I know now
that you know
that we both know
it's only a question of time.

It's a question of time before
you slow down
and walk this way
before you start
whispering in my direction
our direction, as it was meant to be.

Starting Over
by Jenna Mervis

what if love
dries out your mouth

like too much red wine
or talking through the night?

what if love leaves
your tongue

swollen, stuck
against your palate

and your lips
cracked closed

unable to speak
without tearing?

Morning Work
  by Karin Schimke

We are cocked and angled
together like an African chair,
groin-hinged and eye-locked,
small-talking the sun up.
At the join we are genderless
until – out of two flat triangles –
something flowers at us,
blooms bright as though
our eyes are suns
and it must find light.
We give it light, and we laugh,
and then bury it, lids shut,
so it can seed again.

Day
   by Sarah Frost

As the day, a mango,
sheds its skin
orange light snakes through the wild ginger leaves.

I want to take your loneliness,
I let your body dip into mine
as if I were the sea, and you the swimmer.

See how the clouds are clustered,
seeded with shadows.
They are ready to break open with love.

And the day comes.

Worm music

    by Makhosazana Xaba

I want to dance the tango
'cause my feet are so numb.
I want to dance the tango
'cause my thighs need to thaw,
my neck needs loosening,
my eyes need to see when they look,
my waist needs to know not to waste its twist.

Then, my arms will have no choice but to reach out,
my fingers will know to grasp
and, together,
we can dance
to the rhythm of centipedes.

Transformed

by Jeannie Wallace McKeown

Here beside you
I learn your
secret language,
half-breath gasps,
silk of skin, your
flesh leaping
to my touch.

Anniversary
    by Megan Hall

It burst into the wall above our bed –
a rocket, a bullet, a streak of light.
The wall shook and crumbled, falling away.
The roof took off in fright,
flapping wings of mouldy red tiles.

In the middle of the city, our bed:
dogs barking, drunks stumbling home.

This is where the last two years have brought us:
back to a city street

and you,
trying not to hold my hand.

Nameless Places
    by Karin Schimke

The narrow vertical trough between nose and lip
the skin inside an elbow or tucked behind a knee
the ellipses that snake around the tops of legs
where they join the torso
the valleys between toes
that link of ear to skull behind the lobes
the ridge of finger hold
between eyes –

a topographical lexicon
pauses in unwritten skin.

Let's begin.

Intimate

by Robin Winckel-Mellish

The two of us lying there,
my young hands touching
ebony, a cat licking
and loose as a cheetah
on the run, I was
unfurled sail,
speechless as the sea,
beyond control, breath
stirring the outermost
layer of pearl, nerve endings
thin as a peel of fruit,
the husk of closeness
so delicate it trilled.
Now, old hands
feel out the ghosts
of intimacy, the soft
pelt of animal curled
around inner stone,
as bones eaten clean,
ivory glistening
in the warm shadow
of tenderness.

Beyond touch
    by Arja Salafranca

There are intimacies beyond touch,
I am learning.
There are intimacies that reach beyond trust.
I am trying to remember the lesson
as I lean my face into the softness of your smooth neck,
and feel you pulling back
into the responsibilities of your life.
So instead we talk,
about parents, my mother's failing eyesight,
and solutions that *will* appear,
even if we have no idea how.
Of babies, adoption, hot December nights,
a future that mirages into the present.
I try to claim them, lay a stake for the future
as I say goodbye, we kiss lightly on the lips.
And I'm gone, trying to hold you,
hold your words, your thoughts, your face
as the tyres slip past you,
you nesting somewhere in me.

Intact
    by Joan Metelerkamp

we are back
to back
you sink in
to sleep

I am lying as still as I can trying to still my sleeplessness
I feel the breathing wall of you that's why I married you I say

to die with
completely
contradictory
as always
as always
to live with
you say
though I thought you were asleep

I am the wind you are
the grass blown back the grass I am
the grass you are the wind blown back the wind

To the Sisters
    by Dawn Garisch

who keep vigil in the light-drained hours
strung like a rosary: hail mary full of grace

you were with me, blessed was I
amongst women as I waited

alone for my firstborn to tear from my body,
my milk white in the vast dark of his night;

alone for my bruised and fallen son
to choose, nailed between death and life;

alone and home, sick with waiting,
his grasp as slender as the reed of his throat;

alone while other women raise elated faces
to men, then fall back empty, waiting

alone at home with their tender sons while men
rise to penetrate the night – and walk away.

To a friend, on getting older
   by Megan Hall

Beloved, unlike me, you're getting older.
As the sun draws wrinkles with a steel-nibbed pen
and catches the backs of your ears,
and the women with which you enliven your nights,
and afternoons, are younger and younger,
and you older and hairier,
I hope you grow to be a really mean motherfucker,
and travel far, but stay close, and regret me always.

Foundation

by Phillippa Yaa de Villiers

When his wife finally told the truth that she didn't love him anymore,
and maybe she never had, the house stood up and walked away
with the pavement, concrete skirts swishing weirdly in the wind.
He alone in the cold gash in the ground, a worm exposed by the garden spade
white as a root and astonished. The shout froze in his mouth.
The knell   of steps   walking away   with his life,
waning like the moon, she stood on the stoep, weeping like a politician;
waved with one hand and with the other picked up
a fist-sized howling barking hairless red muscle,
wearing a gold collar and leash
and that's when he looked down;
realized the hole in his chest
raw as the one he was standing in.
He shouted and screamed as the house turned the corner
and moved on;
sobbing over and over
she took the dog as well
the bitch.

Seven year itch

 by Azila Talit Reisenberger

"And God has finished on the seventh day His work which He had made, and He rested..." (GENESIS 2:2)

"Six years shall your slave serve you and in the seventh he shall go out free..." (EXODUS 21:2).

In the seventh year
he rested
from all his work and family,
washed his hands,
packed a suitcase,
and
left.

Diary of a relationship

by Kerry Hammerton

It happened on a Monday: heels
head tumble over: my grey eyes
blue, slow your smile; streaked
hair sun my; your lashes long.

On Tuesday I knew the regiment
your granddad served in during
the war, the name of your childhood
pet, a diamond sparkle on my finger.

On Wednesday it was confetti,
a white dress, you intoxicated from
your bachelor party, tolling church bells.

On Thursday a promise
of a child that slipped away,
never to be conceived of again.

On Friday we travelled overseas,
indulged at the spa, reached
a truceful companionship,
tried to harmonise diaries.

Saturday: tears
voices raised,
mysterious
disappearances.

On Sunday I woke up,
forty years old, single
again, you becoming
a dad for the first time.

Geweld / Violence by Karin Schimke

Geweld

gee my 'n mes
laat ek jou uit my vlees kan kerf
laat ek jou soos murg uit my beendere kan skraap
en elke letter van jou heilige naam met 'n lem kan ontskryf.

Violence

give me a knife
to carve you from my flesh
to scrape you from my bones like marrow
and unwrite every letter of your holy name with a blade.

Another North
by Dawn Garisch

I am turning from you
my body swivelling magnetic to another north.

I'm turning to the constant pull
that once wore your countenance,
turning away from the bay of you
nosing out into seas ploughed by storms
I'm sailing into drowning
with a packet of kissed earth stitched to my naked hip
threaded through my bone.

How Healed

by Karin Schimke

How easy now the weight of you
I albatrossed my neck around
and lightfoot heave your heavy heart
that hurt my hollow dead.
How now like lye and bleach
the words that stunned the prose,
that purpled, that tongued –
how bleak I lunged. My love –
I thought I'd die.   How livid
I lived that vice that grip
that terrible, that ship
that rocked alone in
far-from-shore in water drought,
the short and endless parch –
that lip. How the water
the wash the words the weather
the wait healed the hurt, the heavy.

How light now my heels.
How bleached your treason.

letting go

by Colleen Higgs

You can have a perfect afternoon up on a hill, above a valley, it can be overcast, full of love, the grass ripe and if you lie on your back you can see the sky through the grass, and it's like seeing the face of God, and still and yet, you know you have to let go, you sit above the railway line and hear sheep across the way bleating and you also bleat, loudly in different octaves. It's like waiting – sitting there, not for the train to come, because it's already come and gone, not for night to fall, because it will, not for it to start raining, not really for anything, just for itself, waiting for a bit of time to pass and because there isn't anywhere you'd rather be just then, than exactly there, and then it becomes time to go, to get up and he knows it too. The two of you walk to the car, parked at the gate, you cross the tracks, climb through the fence, open the car door, let him into the passenger seat, call the dog to get in too and then you drive home. And it's evening, sunset, and there are the animals to feed and the hose to move to the next pecan tree and supper to eat. And all the while your heart is breaking and you can't breathe, because you know you have to let go, because you can't carry on like this, you can't write or breathe like this, there aren't enough empty spaces, blank pages, open hours, and you need them like you need water and air, and yet your heart which you didn't think could break again, is breaking and you know that you have to let it, you have to let go, because you can't do otherwise, the dreams of choking won't subside, and you know that you won't live or work in strength, if you don't let go, and you don't want to, but you know you have to, and you love him so, love how your bodies fit together, love his tender vibrating hands and his lips, and the energy coursing in his body, you love him and you have to let go, you don't know why, just that you do, and you think of the face of God, the grass on the hillside, the clouds, and the line of the hill, and of all the beauty that is there for its own sake and of all the suffering. And you think that the earth is our mother, our old mother who holds us to her breast even when we bite and kick and deplete her, still she holds us in strong arms, her heart beating, her heart breaking in love and suffering and she's very old, almost eternal.

Night birds

by Arja Salafranca

The night birds trill past midnight.
You hold my fingers in yours
for a long time.
There are no words left.
You have your back turned.
I listen to the birds.

Paper boat
    by Robin Winckel-Mellish

I could have thrown
        all to the wind. Forgotten

the sleepless night
        my foxy odour

mud on the kitchen floor.
        Instead, when you pull

me down, I'm holding myself
        a paper boat on a roaring pond

set to yield by the spillway.

What I want is to say: *Look here*
        knees, breasts, *let go*.

Folding

by Joan Metelerkamp

Side-striped jackal grey as just before dawn
hyena sniffing the vast scent
of what has gone what is to come
lion patched with ash basking in black
in mid-day lala palm
retrorse-eared roan share the reservoir;

subtly, subtly   we repeat ourselves like trees
like northern mopanis   tracts   burnt
trunks like chimneys smoking through the whole bole
we die singly   why should we want to be new –
why be afraid
of repeating ourselves –

like folded rhinoceros   we collapse
in what's left   of the shade

Fragments: Weekend Mythos
by Tariro Ndoro

pick a **colour**   blue   the colour of ocean of water of vast expanses and perhaps   escape
Rusape Dam rushing like blur before the girl's eyes to   the place where time stops still   home

pick a **colour**   white   of white boats, white yachts and pillowy sails   of the people who swim
there   the glistening of fishing rod twine where the girl wants to swim but she is told the river
holds secrets   the dam is a crucible of ~~mermaids~~ menfish

and time stands still

            screams backwards backwards until Max the taxi driver brings her back to her
grandmother's greeting "wauya mwana wa mwanangu, flesh of my flesh" and everything is like
it was *before*

In the shadow of Tsanzaguru and the lion head Tikwiri

pick a **smell**   wet stones   of women hitching their skirts to wade in the river   of Perfection™
soap, greased onto shirts by women speaking freely   a dialect so rare it will be ridiculed out of
the girl's mouth in later years

pick a **smell**, then, acrid (*wet*) cattle rushing to kick their feet in the dip brown black mottled hides and curved horns an excursion soon to be outgrown, along with the climbing of kopjes

pick a **smell** acrid (*dry*) of the library her grandfather left behind shelves that still carry Hemingway & Emecheta but zvipfukuto have eaten the pages the plots have holes in them now bags of fertilizer keep the pages company

pick a **sound** a clang metal on metal iron sharpens iron cow bells on beasts coming home as the orange sun sets

pick a **sound** laughter two sisters playing skip rope in the dust till their feet are brown and ashy on their tongues – a borrowed song that never made sense:

Christopher Columbus was a great man / he went to America in a saucepan / he went to untie, untie, untie / bandy over / two little sausages in a saucepan / one was rotten… / and another went to die!

into supper by firelight orange flames and cricket song wood smoke has burnished the walls remember the girl of those nights where the milky galaxy of bright stars shone sometimes blue sometimes bright and sometimes shooting across the sky (make a wish! make a wish!) then to gossip and prayers and an hour of radio one zvizvizo announcements of births and deaths.

99

pick a **sight**   big silver old moon in the inky black night   hanging like low fruit, ripe for picking

how does the story go?   old Rozvi kings tried to steal it from the heavens   a legend as ancient

as granite

In the shadow of Tsanzaguru and Mount Tikwiri

pick a **smell**   wet earth   wet grass   early morning dew   cow dung and clean smoke

pick a **colour**   pink   frock   Sunday best   follows her grandmother   her grandmother in

Anglican blue in Anglican white in swift gait   a surprise baptism: glacial water on the

girl's forehead   your name is now Theresa Maria Patricia the girl forgets her new

moniker

a particle, **dust,**   gathers on the baptismal certificate   now folded   now carefully placed

in the cardboard box labeled *Envelopes of Tudor*   wherein lies the last image of a long-dead

grandfather   last seen alive in the summer of seventy six

cause of death: unknown

Bequest
    by Beverly Rycroft

for Georgia

Not my headaches
or thin skin,
not the other
sinister genetic thing.

Just more of what
you already have:

laughter
good friends
my love
this poem.

Waning
    by Ingrid Andersen

The moon's silver
has slipped into my curls.
Her shadows deepen
round my eyes
in lines of smiles.

The woman in the mirror
is more my mother than the child inside.

Within Reach
  by Margaret Clough

As age shortens my spine
and makes my fingers curl,
the edges of my life draw inwards.
Possessions lose their meaning.
I leave a roomy house
for a cramped cottage; soon
four walls will close me in and
all that I need will be
only an arm's reach away.

passer-by
  by Marike Beyers

old man in a hat –
fist in my chest
it cannot be him

was he ever that old –
when I think of his voice
I hear a boy on a bike

see his smile bending
over a piece of wood
the sweetness of a day

I walk with his hands
unfolding puppets
as if that could recall him

the unbending thumb
the cracks across knuckles
no winter could reach

Heritage

by Azila Talit Reisenberger

The robe which I have inherited
from my parents
hangs
in the entrance hall.
Still,
I am too small to reach it.

Funeral Sounds
  by Katleho Kano Shoro

Funerals sound like wailing
hearts throbbing, aching
ripping, letting pain in
and allowing it to drip, flow and pour
out of corners of eyes and every tearing pore.

Funerals sound like Sesotho
like accents that travelled from Lesotho
condolences spoken in presence as a show of botho.
They sound like chu-chu-chugging trains, delayed planes
and quiet homes suddenly bursting with dialects from Bloemfontein.

Funerals sound like dithoko. Mouthfuls.
Praise poems whispered to restless bulls.
They sound like the sacrifice's final bellow and the breath it pulls
before exhaling its spirit into the arms of the deceased
personally reciting her through her own ancestry.

Funerals of Bakwena sound like rain
like thunder echoing the survivors' pain
drops of blood and water swirling soil into fane.
Funerals sound like droplets colliding and colluding with tears
the relief of strengthened ancestry clashing with our mortal fears.

Funerals sound like triangles, drums le diphala
'Ndikhokhele' hummed to antagonise the obituary reader.
Difla. High-octane 'koloi ya Eliya!'
They sound like singing your grandmother's favourite hymn
your voice pleading with her keeper to just 'Let. Her. In!'

I quite prefer the funeral sound
to the days after, when you're mourning-bound.
Mourning sounds too much like quietening,
like loneliness persisting,
things unsaid, time unticked and life missing.

For Mme Mmaseliane Mpho Elizabeth Ngatane

The disappearance of the dead
by Megan Hall

For my mother: M H K | 10.10.1940–16.4.1972

I
Where do they go, the dead?

The stories speak of triple-headed hell-hounds with open maws,
burning pyres, towers where the vultures come,
the sad wandering of ghosts in never-nether-worlds.

But you have seeped away into the world;
I cannot find you. Perhaps if I could look
with my father's eyes, I'd see you in the mirror.

Or if your mother hadn't thrown away
the reels that captured you, I could've seen you move.
But there's no chance of that, and anyway,

I want to see you for myself,
not through the filter of someone else.

2
All this suggests a presence you can't have.
For the cremated, the unspoken,
there's no grave to visit, no place to stand and think:

She's here below. Here people stood,
watched the coffin being lowered,
said prayers, threw in soil that landed with a rattle on the lid.

Comforted each other, went home for cake and tea,
then went on grieving: the first Christmas, the first birthday alone,
an empty place each evening, an empty chair.

Friends coming by, looking sorry, speaking her name,
offering to take the children for a night,
bring round a pot of stew –

But here I must break off.   There are no *children* in this case,
only me, and even in a fantasy, I can't picture the life that this implies:
dinner every evening, then TV; being looked after by my dad;

my mother's name spoken in the course of conversation
– with sadness, with regret – but spoken all the same.
This was your mother's favourite sauce; that kind of thing.

It couldn't happen.   The children of suicides don't get
this kind of solicitude. They get another kind: the kind
that watches over them with loving, tender, and careful, eyes,

just in case there's something to *inherit* after all.
No, better to say nothing, better to *keep it quiet.*
Encourage everyone to pretend that nothing's missing,

that there's nothing to miss, everything's all right.

3
What's the answer here? How can I bear a grudge against those
who gave me love, with a sense of taint, love
beyond themselves and their limitations?

4
To my mother, again
A suicide cannot be buried in a churchyard. So I think of you
lingering in the outer reaches, sacrament-less, far from grace,
like Tess's sad daughter, and her wooden cross.

Ground away into the soil, fragments and sensations
frittering away like dust on the wind,
slowly eaten by the moths of forgetting.

Yet you remain, while time holds,
                              mother.

Elegy For Paul
by Jenna Mervis

(for Paul, d.12.06.2009 in Helmand province, Afghanistan)

In this cradle of hills
they still march
their Queen-beat
stiff-arm
rifle-flagging march
that hooked you,
pulled you
into poppy fields.

I see you now before me
would touch your face
this June day.
But you are gone
to ground.

A trumpet wails.
Remember Soho, Paul?
Remember
whiskey-tripping tongues
and drawn-out minors
marooning us at that table?
We jazzed and dreamed
of being poets
and novelists
and famous.

Shots slam the sky
seven soldiers salute
your new station
beneath our feet.

You've gone to ground
today Paul
to the sound of *Yitgaddal veyitqaddash*
we've laid you down.

I'm wearing black for you
today Paul,
its hue ironed
on my tongue.

The Home Bringing

by Robin Winckel-Mellish

We wondered, months later,
whether we'd done right by him,
by not moving him out
through a hole in the wall
of the house so he wouldn't
remember the way back;
not taking the zigzag path
to the burial site, throwing
sharp thorns on the way
so that he wouldn't become
a wandering ghost.
None of this had we done,
no ash smeared on the windows,
the photographs not turned,
how would he have received
a new body to enable him
to move about his world?
Left behind, we didn't forget
the world's a light and living place,
knew he'd be happy to
lightfoot the journey,
so we feasted and sang,
remembering the way
the passage of time
had worked on him,
and declared our faith
in the world of the perishable,
the great wound staining us all,

the slain ox bringing him
back home to his family,
and we pressed our lips
into the earth, weighted
our voices with silence,
grasped the past's
transcendent dust.

Two poems by Malika Ndlovu

12th March, 09h35

Cigarettes put me in touch with my pain
Catch my breath
Coat my throat
I wrap my feet in new shoes,
My overweight body in new clothes
Dark and discreet.
Hair uncovered,
Toenails deep red,
Frida Kahlo feelings bleed
Into my heart and head.

28th April, 22h45

My lower back remembers. My breasts remember. My feet
remember. When I see the thin film of sweat on my forearms,
my eyes linger on the hair there. Your fragile forearms were
covered with fine hairs too, an obvious beautiful affirmation that
you came from me. The air I breathe thickens with memories.

another country
    by Colleen Higgs

When my father died
I crossed into another country,
more human than the one I'd left behind.

It's easier to travel by foot.
People take time to greet each other.
The only food is mealie meal and vegetables.
It's a poor country.

The past was too bright, too hot, too white.
What's left over, left behind
is a long piece of string.

It's almost impossible
to find out the truth
but we keep going, as though
motion itself will save us.

If I lose my foothold
there's no-one here
to catch me.   I'll fall
forever.

ou werf
by Thandi Sliepen

all the turtles
are flying to the moon
martin do you see them
once you gave me a cave
to live in and now
you are like the ferryman
to the land of cadmium
lemon hue

all the turtles
are leaving i see them
silhouetted wings in the sky
and you so stern
now i pray may i see
wings on all our
ancient backs

in memoriam

by Elisa Galgut

in the first dream, you're consumed
with illness, a caricature, the shadow
of a flightless bird, the skeleton
of a bird fossilised in stone.
in the other, you're in the kitchen,
standing by the sink washing dishes.
you're wearing your blue night gown;
you're ill but i am overjoyed to see you.
i can feel, even in sleep, the jolt of joy,
the unexpected sight of your appearance.
in both dreams you're alive
and i know that i'm dreaming;
i know you'll be gone when I awake.
i'll lose you, once again, to the daylight –
     my waking will kill you.

Wearing Silence
by Michelle McGrane

On the day of your funeral
the air hums; everything is green.

I sprawl on the lawn in the sun,
wearing silence

        and watch
a small white butterfly flutter by

through the vault of old oaks
and up over the garden wall.

Penelope
    by Joan Metelerkamp

If I were a woman working
    a myth I could make my own –

making, unmaking,
    all that stuff
    repeating
    whatever you read about a woman writing
what does it matter
            I could simply say undoing
                unravelling
    unconscious –

(this sun: leaching all the energy out of me
and head aching, sun: I need shape, form, I need dream, sun,
I need help).

A book, like the bookclub ladies' books
Joan, why don't you write a book?

If I were a woman working
          who could answer

why do you think Penelope pulled out all that knitting
every evening
creeping, unheard, unweaving

every morning
back to the first line –

do we even know what she was making?

The pure necessity – a shroud
              for the old king

what was it, king,
what was the image ingrained,
what was the feel, the form,
the ecphrasis,

the work of art, in other words, within the work of art?

Imagine it, what was it was woven,
woven together as unanswerable riddles?

The train went over the bridge
What was the driver's name?

Driven by the question

Penelope all day at it all night
with her handmaid
pulling it all out
like a nightmare, a dream anyway, where you never get anywhere

only eventually
over twenty two years...

Perhaps, my daughter suggests (perhaps she only imagines it),
what she was weaving, Penelope: the story of Odysseus –
to bring him back –
her own story in other words
to make the masculine more secure

couldn't she weave
to save her life
to save his life
she took it all out again –

you've written yourself
and written yourself off
a long time –

head still aching its head off:
burnt out like the modem blitzed by lightning
(like a fool I left it plugged in)

*

Head stuck in the fence, will utterly undirected
afraid of the hard and strong
unable to turn this way or that
since Sunday –

sheep with its head in the fence
or rooikat

after you'd eaten forty lambs and my brother finally caught you
and caged you – bleeding
above your right eye
(taken you off to the Tsitsikamma and don't be a bloody fool
and come back).

Shall I pull it all out, my knitting, I thought –
I woke this morning thinking of knitting: like a picket fence
needles pulled out
fence of rib with the loops all loose –
imagine walking around with that on your back, wrote Anne Sexton –
imagine walking around with a picket fence
(only I didn't see it – my head's been stuck in it since Sunday)
Anne Sexton's letters I've been stuck in them since Sunday
acting upon me *like a misfortune*
serving *as an axe*
leaking all over the page bleeding to hell and gone –

I dreamt a little blue car
"whose car is that" I woke thinking, forgetting
my own
"bloo jool" I thought "it's Anne Sexton's"

but it was trapped under a timber truck
could anyone have got out alive
no no no no no
       it is impossible!
              get out of there alive!

there is a long thin fury
　　　　whacking a plank
　　　　　　　fallen from the truck

get out of there!
　　　　she strikes the truck –
　　　　hits back –

*

I can tell you
it wasn't my weaving that saved me –
if you can call this saved
sometimes I think I'm finished with that –
will I go back,
is it finished or not?
All that doubt, all that sweat
with the fucking suitors –

it was my son, it was Telemachus, obviously,

going off to parties, yes, and singing in rock concerts
and all the girls all round him and always
on the phone to his friends who haven't listened in class
and preparing
for his last tests
and nervous
and tired
of being the only responsible one and president of the SRC –

but I'm his mother after all
and I can tell you something
(as I told my friend and she said:
"isn't that *dependence*"
but actually this is my odyssey)

when I look at him I see
                  he needs me
not fussing obsessing counting and keeping

calm down, mother, take it easy –

what he needs
                  is my faith
as the fates say
that's all, really, he needs nothing of me.

                  *

When the old king lies in his sick bed
waking from a dream cries
'you are free, free – let your son
go off and become an artisan'

I dismiss my first thought –
is this your way of dissing my son
your refusal to see he's a prince – your grandson –

instead I thank him –
he's saying: you are living as you choose –

but the weight of his words, like
make something
of all the old responsibility picked up and carried
since my last year at school
of those to whom much is given much will be required

earlier, thirteen when I learnt the words
for the part I had by heart
o my father, had I the tongue of Orpheus
to make the stones to leap and follow me....
do not take away this life of mine
before its dying time —

take myself to bed with my ten day aching head
and vertigo, let the world spin;
and as I lie there watching the wind as I lie there –
nothing –
who sees the wind after all?

*

All this energy all this endless spinster-like activity
trying to keep myself together – for what –
for nothing, for breaking with pain spinning
            out of control
there was nothing else for it.

When he gets back he lies like Odysseus
on my bed in my workroom and cries –
he doesn't even know which lines have moved him
he doesn't really know why; he knows why
I've been working
he is so exhausted – all of it – we had to do it –

*

Penelope: perhaps like the wicked queen
she wasn't on the right side of those little impulses,
the ones who would have finished her work for her –
or even like the young queen
wanting to keep her king and her baby
if she weren't obsessively looking at herself in the mirror splitting
hairs, splitting
apart every night;
if she could just have let it be
sleeping, dreaming

if she weren't wanting to make it all the time
if she weren't worrying about her husband
this weaving of heroes and heroic dissent and descent and constant
contest and success –
or even if she weren't so determined every day
as if she were going out to find food while he wandered!
to fish, say, for her family

cast on cast off, drop, pick up, carry,

if she just allowed a little more slack if she afforded a little more give
if she let the lines rest a little, released, delivered like *I fish in your give.*

We have lived from
birth in this fist of
rock / and ocean

Across the River Kei
by Sindiwe Magona

Land of low skies, far horizons;
Sunrises that glow low steeples,
Paint cow horns above still
Far-from-discernible bodies
Huddled close in the morning kraal,
Chewing yesterday's cud as sun's early rays
Listen to the satisfied moos of cows
All heralding the dawn; early sun
Buttering morning clouds,
Bidding lovers disengage.

The Girl from Qumbu
   by Christine Coates

Thatched huts on the hills
the eyes of speckled cattle;
these are the shapes of her childhood –
the girl from Qumbu.

A cowry – it is a darning shell,
it is an ear –
she hears the ocean,
the whispering voices of her grandmothers.

The crack on its underside –
this is where we come into the world –
from the salty sea inside –
the white circles milk makes,
the white enamel bucket.

This brown and spotted shell
the hides of Nguni cows,
the headlamps of her dad's Humber
the shade of the amber tree –

like a tadpole finds its way out –
she breaks open.

Kalahari Blue

by Robin Winckel-Mellish

Here there is nothing but Camel Thorn trees. Crumpled shadows
enfold the low scrub, then the rural dwellings and chicken coops,
a pale shell in an ocean of bushveld. The day's heat subsides and
the sisters welcome the gloam, a visible spectrum between green
and indigo. In the house the music player is turned on and the
microphone connected. Outside the night sky begins its glitter,
fireflies have reached the Milky Way. Two frail sisters put on frocks,
carefully comb hair. They will sing the one song they are good at,
the only song they remember: *Blue on blue, heartache on heartache* ...
As if tracking a Kudu they spear memory into music. Bruised shades
of melody lift, as if a sea of driftwood is rolling. Turning, pushing
forward, pulling back. The karaoke sounds grow louder, the cadence
heavier. Somewhere in the shadow a hyena is laughing. Whoops as
she brings down an antelope, sings as she tears the flesh, finds the
chamber of its heart. Drags the carcass to her den like a sack of love.

School mornings before a test
 by Christine Coates

Footsteps of the milkman,
the clink of bottles –
I'm up early to study;
it's cold here in the Western Transvaal,
the light a dirty grey,
the unlikely hum of the milk cart,
its battery engine
down the street –
milk and orange juice.
Cars start up – dads taking kids to school,
maids walk from the bus stop
calling to one another
as they peel off into
individual driveways.

my Yeoville
by Colleen Higgs

Where were you when you could play
freedom fighter, a dangerous game,
a particular way
of being worried about spies?
And who was really ANC and who wasn't.

And we danced. The Lurchers. The Yeoville Rapist.
Weird and wild and strange. Sex, drugs.
Because I lived there it was wonderful,
and the library, Tandoor, the Harbour, Midnight Express
Elaines, Rumours, Mamas.
The park at night, the path, the plane trees
the police station. Yeoville Checkers.

Bigger and wider and smaller my world was then
realised how much and how many
were mostly Zulu speakers
and so many who didn't speak any English. Only Serbian.
Any night of the week on Rockey Street
there wasn't one uniform
if you liked, you could fit in.
You could go and experience something–
come in from the cold
from Alberton, Kempton Park.

By the mid 90s the banks started redlining,
kickstarting slumlording.
You could hear buses changing gear
from the bedroom at Homelands.
One day the swimming pool opened to all.

Steak
    by Arja Salafranca

For Don and Sue

There's a perfection in the sharp knife,
handle thick and satisfying to hold.
It eases through the meat, parting it
like the Red Sea.
A thin trail of red juice eases out,
I spear the soft buttery steak
with a mushroom, add a half-moon of avocado,
a quartered tomato.
The food shatters in my mouth.

There's something about summer nights,
the kind of nights that follow days
in a city that reeks of boiled bodies
crisping under the sun's glare.
There's something: the lack of breeze,
the water in the pool gleaming bluely,
the soft murmur of traffic.

It's an island, an oasis, the lawn jewelled green.
Candles illuminate our faces
the silver, the sparkling cutlery,
the sheer perfection of knife, fork, crystal glass,
steak, salad, speared food, shattered tastes.
At the bottom of a garden,
in the heart of Johannesburg.

Dancing on Robben Island
   by Megan Hall

after a visit to KwaMuhle Museum, Durban, March 2004

I
Govan Archibald Mvuyelwa Mbeki, born 1910,
of the Mfengu people, and the Zizi clan,
married Epainette Moerane.

Between 1933 and 1937, he read
penny Lenin texts bought at
The People Bookshop in Braamfontein.

He was 'a ballroom dancer of some repute'.
Together, 'they danced the quick step and the tango
at a club they started in Durban.

Later, alone in his prison cell
on Robben Island, he would rehearse those steps,
and imagine: Ma Mofokeng,

smiling in his arms.'

2

In her navy and black clothes,
Epainette feists through her glasses at the camera.
Her demeanour says, *No compromise.*
Says, *I am here in Idutywa to stay.*

No matter that her husband
(yes, they're still married),
the well-regarded Govan, has gone to Cape Town
to live a life of urban ease.

Her glance still says: *Here
there is something I can achieve.*

now me heads

   by Thandi Sliepen

are stretching apart
reflections in an intercape
double bubble plastic bus
but i take
the free drink

blurred water joints
ductile fontanels
sticking together
i am hanging from the ceiling
every turn and glance outside
spilling the fake fruit juice
sucking me brains ever thinner
sinewy connections

flying guillotines
it's a warning
gliding past white houses
overseeing white beaches
broken necks absurdly strolling
in severed tranquillity
onward on this journey of separation
wearing our shades
away from the bleached bays
a dip in the tarmac
all the heads in rows slip grip
only just remaining attached

inland the passing township
kids so far from the sea
superimposed on our hidden heads
a synthetic pane screening today
splitting bodies on
carved up land

The way light falls
   by Haidee Kotze

It's Wednesday and
the sky has
a biblical look
to it, like
a prophet's beard
straggling red over
the horizon. She
picks up her
weight and walks
through the gate,
into the morning.
Her body disappears
but she leaves
tracks in the
mud: an invitation
for hunting. In

the street children
cling to the
pavement while their
mothers unplug themselves
from the day
ahead. The wind
sleeps between buildings.
She watches the
chickens like 3D-mosaics
behind wire, and
wonders about feathered

things and how
to kill them.
She buys a
remote control and
notes the particular
taste of milk
and metal on
her tongue, and
thinks: none of

us understand our
breathing, still we
breathe; still we
remember how a
kiss can turn
you into a
stranger to yourself.
Yes, there is
redemption in this,
she says to
her belly: the
way light falls
on hands here.

Sign Poem 34

by Eliza Kentridge

His body in disarray
Like something shaken up in a bag
On the way home from the shops
Man or boy?
I couldn't say
Arranged on the pavement
Arms, legs, elbows, feet
Nothing in the right place
A bag of bones thrown together by a witchdoctor
A suitcase of a human
Badly damaged in transit

BUT TO WHOM COULD HE WRITE?
DEAR SIR, I WISH TO COMPLAIN

He was uncomplaining
I remember him smiling and talking
I think he had a companion
Someone must have helped him
Assembled him on his spot under the portico
Because there he was

DAD, WHAT'S WRONG WITH HIM?
THE FRIGHTENING ERRORS OF THE BODY

On the pavement,
Cardboard for a cushion
We put coins in his hat

Visiting you at work
Up in the lift to the Sixth Floor
Past the receptionist
The secretary
Past other lawyers who made comments
Shook your hand
Nodded at us

We followed you into your chambers
That grand word

A KING'S WORD

A wood panelled room
Bookshelves full of law reports
No novels here
Your big desk, some big chairs
A medieval woman looked at us from her panel
Dark eyes in a worn gold frame
And we looked out of the recessed windows
Supreme Court pillared across the road
Advocates in gowns crossing the road
Collared

We tried to find him below us on the pavement
But the angle was wrong
He was under the portico

We jinked about while you gathered papers
Ready for the next thing

A milkshake?
Or a gingerbread man from the OK Bazaars?

Back down and out
Past the bundled man-boy
I drew away into the life you gave me
And here I still am
But where did he go when night came?
Who looked out for him?
What happened to him?
There must have been some human pleasures

THOUGH HE'D BEEN TRAMPLED BY A MONSTER
Crumpled

He had a name which we never thought to ask
All of us there in the same unfair space
Locked apart in the sugared afternoon
Worlds almost impossible to mention

A person
by Ingrid Andersen

Abahlali baseMjondolo
affirms that a person is
a person no matter where
they're from.
Only actions are illegal.

But that's not always how we feel,
wait-listed and angry,
returning, work-clad, to
these shacks on borrowed land.

It's as if the zinc
has sunk into our skin.
We bear this shame
upon our waiting faces.

Retired

by Arja Salafranca

A half-smoked cigarette, the droop of a flabby neck,
wraparound sunglasses,
the skin darkly furrowed by sun.
In her room
she watches soap operas,
the characters become her life.
They are muted by the sun that bleaches
her TV screen to pale, washed-out colours.
She still watches,
struggling against the light.
Her voice is raspy, throaty, blunted by smoking.
There is no point in giving it up now.
There are bars down the road
where she drinks brandy and coke.

It's not an empty life;
there are things to occupy her
on this strip of flats near the sea.
(Living alone the TV is a friend.)
It's a bit of a sad life, at times,
she admits, but not so sad she'd want to
go back to working,
and tallying up figures
for someone else in an office.
It's an okay life at 62.
What else can you expect?

4.00 am
by Michelle McGrane

The young mother rises in silence
from the rough pinewood pallet on the floor.
Curled together under their musty, grey blanket,
the children breathe easily and do not stir.
She, a stooped shadow groping in darkness,
draws the darned widow's dress
over her bony shoulders and chest –
inhaling her body's odour –
covering the grape-sized sores on her legs.
All around she hears the rustling presence
of the watchful, impassive dead.
She rubs her tired eyes and coughs. Sharply.
The small mud hut is sour, airless.
Her captured lungs are intricate knots.
She leaves two, sticky-soft bananas
on a scratched plastic plate for when they awake.
In the chill of morning, she latches the door
and sets out north, along a narrow dirt road,
twelve kilometres over precarious farmland,
to the crammed, weekly government clinic.
From down here, in the crowded bone valley,
Saturn rides high in the sky.
The air is swollen with damp earth and lantana.
She walks slowly, softly humming a hymn
while the cold wind flutters the ends
of her gaily-patterned headscarf.

Gangster's paradise
by Shirmoney Rhode

Is swaa' om te droem as djy 'n kopseer het,
uncle Piet en Jannie se button pype maak my naar,
antie Malla agter innie jaart se gesig
wanne sy nie wiet wat hulle gaan iet'ie,
maak my moeg.
Die gunskote klink al soes music
in 'n sad play waa' jong laities altyd die prey is,
alles gie my 'n kopseer
en is swaa' om te droem as djy 'n kopseer het.

Jozi parks

by Phillippa Yaa de Villiers

Smashed beer bottles don't give a damn
about barefoot children. Adults, swollen
with disappointment, sit sadly in the swings.
They've got their own problems: they are empty now
and useless; most of the time, shattered and discarded.
Children come uninvited, so let them cut their feet:
we all learn through pain. We were the same.
They'll grow up make the same mistakes
that we did again.
Our parents also saved up and bought us shoes
and still we limp home.

History
   by Dawn Garisch

As a child I pictured the history of Africa:
Dingaan betraying Piet Retief
at dinner. Today in my son's textbook
I see how a black man sits
and looks sits and looks
at two objects lying at his feet.
You can tell by the hunch
of his shoulders, by the way his hands hang
slack; you can tell by the faces
of the other black men standing round, helpless –
look at him: look: look this man failed,
failed to obtain his quota
on a Congolese rubber plantation. Therefore,
therefore and forever,
he sits and looks sits and looks
at the severed hands of his five-year-old daughter.

A young debriefing for Sankara
by Katleho Kano Shoro

Dear Thomas, Mr Sankara
our visionary martyr
we resurrect your cotton-clad spirit
We, the children of women and workers
whom you once let bloom in it.

The old men who knew how to dye and weave
died and were woven into a typical African story,
the one where the IMF dictates
the Faso Fani factory's suicide.
At least it was nothing like Namibia's hushed genocide.

Ntate Sankara
Black is still poor
women are still war pawns
and our parents forgot to build black industries
– although we have our eyes on Kagame.

Upright Man
now, *we're* trying,
quitting nine-to-fives in pursuit of collective creativity
and our colonial education is burning.
It is we who are building and burning!

Trade Matters
by Isobel Dixon

copal coconuts beeswax ambergris
ivory rhinoceros horn cowrie shell

(also known as blackamoor's teeth)
always be sure to check the teeth

for a slave to snore in sleeping
is counted a very great fault indeed

make them run a little way
there should be no defect of the feet

a child worth a pound or two
in Zanzibar will fetch twenty in Persia

no one buys an adult slave (domestic –
wild from inland is a different matter)

their masters never part with them
till they are found incorrigible

but the wild slaves though saleable
are a source of lawlessness and robbery

the worst is the treacherous weather
the tedium, the wearisome monotony

every merchant hopes to leave
as soon as he can realise a tidy sum

every agent would persuade
his employer to recall him

South African War Horses

by Wendy Woodward

In the South African War
326,073 horses died, 51,399 mules—
and that was on the British side.

They died before they got here
from India, Argentina, Australia.
They died
       in ships,
       at the quayside,
       of disease,
       of neglect,
       on the battlefield.

They elude my imaginings,
these half-million beings.

But before me, an image of revenants
from that war: Privates Makin
and Dean pose on their horses in
the bright Molteno sunshine.
Makin's face is shadowed,
a metaphor, perhaps, for what is to come.
Dean's jaw tenses away from our gaze.
They have rifles in their right hands,
cartridge belts bisect their chests.
They lack bravado, these young men;
they do not scoff at their fates.
Their horses are vulnerable, too:

they half-close their eyes to the glare,
their stories already written on their bodies.

Makin's bay lacks muscle
and his tail is docked like that of a *kripvreter*,
cossetted in a stable.
Dean's dappled grey will stand out in rifle sights
from dawn to dusk
and in moonless dark, too.

In this image they remain alive.
The bay muses on the present moment.
The grey flicks her ears to the rider.
Their bodies warm in the midday sun,
their stories, shadowed, directly beneath them
in the quiet, prescient sand.

The Boer horses had already set
their hooves down, below *krantzes*,
over khaki stones
and through *spruits*.
Statistics do not tell
how many of them
collapsed from starvation or exhaustion,
their farms burnt in the veld.

Their names enliven their markings,
their belligerence, their beauty:

Viljoen's *Blesman*, Reitz's *Malpert*, Visser's *Voorslag*,
de Wet's *Fleur*, de la Rey's *Starlight*, Malan's *Very Nice*.

Yet names were no charms
against death,
which came for them soon enough.
Sixty ponies of the Groot Reent Kêrels
died in an ice storm, leaving the men
grieving with saddles in a night
branded forever
by their loss in the killing rain.

Each autumn, old battlefields
come alive with the colour of cosmos,
flowers from the droppings
of horses who ate seed
from Mexico, and beyond
more than a hundred years ago –
little pennants in a remembering wind.

the women with steel necks
    by Thandi Sliepen

do you walk
miles for water
the earth fuelling your beauty
through the dry cracks
and moulded arch of your soles

the women with steel necks
are passing
faded plastic buckets
are passing turning
around cool liquid bricks
as heads revolve to laugh and joke
retracing steps
in an endless curved landscape
anguine passage between
thighs land and sky

to know the weight
of every drop
precious pillars of salt
the women
with steel necks are passing

The leader
   by Sindiwe Magona

Inspired by the photographs of UN photographer John Isaac

Rake thin, this old woman
At the head of a straggling line.
Eye fixed on distant horizon,
Strides along the famished road.
The corpses she'll feed it behind her;
Disciples going toward the Cross;
Pilate, the men Africa calls leaders.

Spit not swallow
    by Katleho Kano Shoro

Drink up!
Know what bitterness swirls in your mouth.

Spit it out!
We have become too comfortable with swallowing disasters.

Unlikely
 by Colleen Crawford Cousins

My great great great grandfather
in 1820   a pale boy on a ship
silenced by his mother's groans   seasick all of them
the Cape of Storms and then the journey up the shipwrecked coast
the savage stories of the sailors   the food
the rankness below   he saw a whale breach
too many porpoises finning
leaping through the unending sea with a terrible purpose
the strangely human eyes
(Baines has painted the arrival
a rowing boat   green breakers   beached)
East London a rough town
cobbled streets   the Quigney
the hostile faces of the porters
clicking in their gabble   smelling of wood smoke
the hard sky intolerably blue   intolerable

His father said
we are here to build this country up   unlikely
he thought

Rock fig

by Karin Schimke

Tell them it's not just me who grows root-wild around the boulder
of this koppie. Exotic once and now endemic, we're all stubborn, but
unimportant. Ignore us. Long after they've cut us loose, we'll clench these
places in our root-fists.

You told me
   by Makhosazana Xaba

You told me you speak French,
took lessons evening after evening.
It was important to you that,
when you go on your dream holiday in Paris,
you can communicate
because the French are hostile
when you do not speak their language.

You told me you speak Yiddish
'cause your grandparents spoke it to you,
you learnt it as a child and, surprisingly,
you still speak it well, decades later.

You told me you've had
Black friends since 1976
since the struggle days
because you were involved
in the struggle for that long.
You drove comrades to their homes
after meetings, at night,
braving the drive back to your own suburb.
You met your comrades' parents, their families.
You even baby sat their children.

You told me that
you loved your nanny with all your heart
because she raised you like her own.
In fact, you told me

you used to run to her
in her servants' quarters, at the back,
when your big house in front felt lonely
and your parents were having a fight.

Yes, you even said,
you said you preferred her company
to that of your parents,
and your parents' friends,
because she sang songs to you,
put you on her lap
and rocked you to sleep
while your family
had arguments around the dinner table.

You have academic degrees,
articles published in peer-reviewed international journals.
You are a true South African who
dedicated your life to the struggle.
You told me you even had Black lovers
because colour never meant anything to you.

You also told me you have taken
so many "Zulu lessons" you have lost count.
But, because the lessons were too didactic,
the language too tonal, time too tight,
struggle meetings took too much time,
you *still* cannot speak isiZulu, or any indigenous language.

Sixty-nine bullets

by Phillippa Yaa de Villiers

(for the Sharpeville 69)

Sixty-nine bodies
caught in half-sentences:

- I was on my way to the shop
- I saw this chap I like
- He's all fire, his skin and eyes
- Are copper weapons, blazing in the turning sun
- I go soft in his hard eyes, can't stop smiling
- Oh, it was still quiet when I came past
- And he told me to go home
- Things could get nasty
- Then he smiled and said
- Let's meet
- Afterwards
- I didn't know the protest was illegal
- But I suppose that's obvious, after all
- Isn't everything we blacks do
- Illegal?
- I tried to get in front of her
- But it was too late
- She fell first
- I didn't want to be a voiceless victim
- I knew exactly what I was getting into
- But she was not supposed to be there
- I was escorting my friend
- He is into this PAC

- My father says we should rather get better jobs than he could
- Who wants to be a matshingilane in Hillbrow
- Some blacks are even lawyers, he says. Why do I pay school fees?
- I told him, this protest is for him too
- He said he's on night shift, he hasn't got time for
- This young boy's nonsense
- He couldn't see his way to be there,
- So I was there for him.
- Me, I was clear in my mind,
- Because I was nineteen
- Robert Sobukwe spoke at our school
- We can only liberate ourselves and it starts here
- It was true, why are we poor tenants of our own
- Inheritance?
- This disorder could only be cured
- By naming it, and inhibiting its spread
- By liberating our minds from its poison
- Hey, death happens to everyone
- We should not take it personally, after all, it was a protest,
- It was political
- We knew what we were doing,
- What is this world we are creating?
- Rather die for freedom than live like a slave
- What will I tell my children when they ask
- Where were you?
- Whatever happens, at least I spoke out
- It was political, I agree
- But death is personal

- Very personal
- Each death as unique as birth
- With its own portents
- And banalities
- Who will fetch the baby from the crèche?
- Who will tell my mother?
- I didn't mean to hurt
- I didn't know what we were doing was so bad
- Oh well, we knew we were risking
- But still
- All my tomorrows
- All my tomorrows, please
- I surrender
- I surrender
- I surrender
- I surrender
- Please, could you stop shooting
- Now?

Nouns

by Isobel Dixon

Roads, Walls

Walls, Roads

Roads, Walls, Flags
Martyrs, Walls, Checkpoints, Flags
Prisoners, Walls, Martyrs, Orphans
Orphans, Widows, Prisoners, Walls

Checkpoints, Walls, Checkpoints

Walls, Shells

Shells, Sons, Walls
Sons, Funerals, Coffins, Flags
Sons

Songs, Sons, Funerals, Shells
Shells, Walls

Talks, Walls, Missiles, Drones
Mortars, Missiles, Drones, Shells
Drones, Airstrikes, Talks, Ceasefire

Airstrikes
Ceasetalks

Airstrikes, Missiles, Drones

Drones, Bulldozers, Tanks

Tanks, Bulldozers

Ceasefire

Talks

Remembering S-21, Cambodia

by Fiona Zerbst

– for Vann Nath

I.
This was a school
before it was wire and silence.

Oleander
scented the sunlit courtyard.

This was a school,
with blackboards, white-

and-tan-tiled floors. Children
filled the concrete stairwells.

Then it was wire, shackles,
prisoners taken

from their families. They were beaten,

starved, herded like children,
helpless, fed a gruel

of watery rice. Obedient,
they still starved.

II.
Vann Nath, the painter,
drew his captor's head.

Kept alive on a whim,
he drew each line

like a precious, living thing.
Each line a lifeline

as long as his captor's
vanity saw likeness there.

III.
A worker told Vann Nath, 'Just let things be.'
'Death stays close to us,' he said. Vann Nath drew

and sculpted. Nothing else for him to do
but stay close to the enemy, keep silent.

IV.
Under the oleander,
in the silence,
it is a lovely garden.
Children must have

played here, enjoyed
the morning sunlight,
before their parents
fetched them; before dark.

Blood Delta

by Dawn Garisch

Last night at dinner around a white linen table,
deep magenta wine held ellipsed in the spill
of light after years of ripening in silence,
a man I know plunged his fork into his lamb
well-marinaded, slow-oven-cooked, and said
he admired Nigeria for hanging Ken Saro Wiwa.
The gravy ran, oil fields spilt their slick. I went home,

and wept for words that have never left my lips
nor fingers. I did not object. My heart kept fisting
my unspilt blood round and round. What use
these hacked marks and scribbles, these clasps
of sound. A frightened man who wields the fork
of power will not be swayed by talk or inky dribbles.

Saro Wiwa said it did not matter if he lived or died,
but that we try to make the world a better place.
Will his blood courage purge the Niger Delta?
What word can change the river of the world?

The offending document

by Tariro Ndoro

It could be any handbag; it could be a messenger bag with extra-long straps, a designer bag with large Louis Vuitton logos or a scuffed black one that looks cheap. Let's assume it is the scuffed black one, it is the one you see most often. We must assume that its owner is stressed – that is how she walks, that is how her nostrils flare. Her hair looks frustrated, that is to say, it was once relaxed, and now it has growth; and since she's been hustled all day, the hair stands on one end. There is sweat on her brow and she is wearing a frock; yes, a frock because it is floral and black and made of cheap rayon. Her outfit is completed by knock-off tennis shoes that are not of the Tommy variety but she still calls them "matomi". Yet this woman is just like the twenty-something woman with dreadlocks (we pray to God she's not smoking mbanje). Her nose has a stud in it, another cardinal sin, and she too is frustrated. This can be attested to because she is telling her boyfriend, quite eloquently, on her iPhone.

It is true the older woman's bag is heavy because of the old Nokia phone she'll never replace, the one ply tissue paper still on its roll (in case she has to use a public toilet) and an old Fanta bottle full of water. Her wallet is just as scuffed as her bag but that doesn't deter her – most of her money is in her bra anyway. The younger woman carries a bottle of mineral water, chewing gum, a book and a passport. It is this document has relegated them to the same fate. For now, the two women might share a camaraderie, a complaining together if you will, but after they've crossed the border, one will head for a bus station in Joburg where she will sleep under a truck for R2 a night until she has enough merchandise to sell at home, the other will take the Gautrain to Marlboro where her aunt lives and spend her days between Gold Reef City and Sandton. For now they are equal because of that offending document.

Land reform
    by Colleen Crawford Cousins

The train to Alicedale
Those clouds
Two blues, a complex grey
Drowse in the crooked mirror of the dam.
Her case is packed for Joburg. A child
Sleeps against the window

Biko – your grave in Ginsburg
Our prayers float up like smoke
Women bitter as salt sit
against the warmest wall
Barefoot in her cloak
Noxolo praises you

Twenty four yokes in an empty house
The oxen are all gone
This earth is furrowed with the dead
I touched your stone cold stone

Rock art site, Salem
I can't touch you mother through this rock
You've died away into the slant of a cheekbone
Your eyes more alien than spaceships
Your hands cup change from cigarettes

Alone on this hill in Salem
My eye catches your creature
Duiker I call in answer to his name

Up here the stars are arrows
behind the winter sun

In your body mother
You flew and swam and spoke with animals
As I do in dreams
Against barbed wire and stagnant water
Tired grasses lean

Salem means broken promises
Twenty six houses mother
Their black mouths gaping saying

Rain taxi school fees pension
Nietverwacht and allesverloren
On the faint radio I pick up through the static
Agrarian tenurial restitution

Truths & Reconciliations

by Isobel Dixon

Pragmatic whitewash,
rainbow complacencies,
the miracles forgot –
but would you forgive the man
who made your father blind?
No single hand put out those eyes,
no blade or burning brand –
but you knew there was an Island,
though you never thought
of the detail at the time:
the slow and bitter years,
the chipped-out days,
the worn-down line of men
bent in the burning sun
to the glitter of the lime.

Eurydice and the TRC
by Elisa Galgut

I knew they'd send him
To woo me back with his music,
His sweet songs, his ardour.
He always could inspire love.

I hear
Melodies that linger like the scent of perfume

And I know he's near
To return me, to take me home.

The bastard.

What does he know, grandson of memory,
Poet of pastures, of this still place?
He thinks we are like the living,
Only dislocated, condemned
To silence, mouths open fishlike without speaking.

The breathless ones.

Here we have nothing to do but forget.
I am drained of memories –
They ooze from every wound,
Leak from any break in skin or bone.
I have bled myself dry of him,
Sweated all caresses, spat out
Every kiss.

I am dismembered; mourning
Is beyond me.

His music will sew me up like a marionette;
I shall caper like a pantomime of my living self
To ease some pain that's nothing,
Anymore, to do with me.
Let the living find their own forgiveness.

Why?

by Isobel Dixon

Because I say so.
The world isn't fair.
Do as I say, not as I do.
Handsome is as handsome does.
Manners maketh the man.
Beggars can't be choosers.
If wishes were horses,
beggars would ride.
The poor will always be with us.
God in His wisdom knows.
Lambda (at present unknown).
Lambda, at present unknown.

The things they do not tell you
by Karin Schimke

Who else remembers the squeak and chafe of the gate,
the hoopoe in the bottlebrush or the way the grass
sank beneath the lightness of your small body's weight?

The hosepipe coiled on the path that lead to the front door,
fading slasto on the stoep, or the crack in the chimney
that grew wider every year as the house sank into the floor?

Unspeakable things were happening not far away
and they never told us. Never spoke of pity or complicity,
never said anything they could later downplay.

Does anyone remember that the brakes on the bike
churred and creaked? Does anyone remember the sound
of their own name in the mouth of their father, or the shrike,

or remember how in the morning each limb on the body awoke
in fear, hope, despair, wonder? Oh come. No one remembers
in abstracts. You like to think you recall the smell of smoke

but you were only eight and there were a hundred kilometres
between the dead child and the patterns you were tracing
on the kitchen linoleum that day long ago one winter.

Don't mention the war

by Phillippa Yaa de Villiers

For C

Don't mention that your grandparents escaped gas ovens, think of something nice to say, anyway it was long ago and you're still here almost! Don't mention the men in balaclavas who beat you and your husband in front of your three-year-old child before locking you in the boot of your car. Crime brings down property values so don't mention it, don't mention Marikana and who gets what, and don't try to come up with a theory or make some claim about the relationship of crime to poverty, you've never been poor so make do with your lot and don't mention the robbers that crossed the double stand adventure garden and forced themselves into the French windows of your three-bedroomed farmhouse and dragged you out of your dream under the duck-down duvet. You pinched your lips together stifled sounds as they manhandled you around the house demanding money and kicked away the teacher's salary in your wallet because it was not enough. Don't mention that you looted your child's money box for the one hundred dollars that her aunt in the US sent to her in increments of ten dollars per birthday and Christmas for the past five years, don't mention them (especially to the child! She'll be FURIOUS). Don't mention that they tied you up and threatened to shoot you (Ag, there was no sign of a gun and they were young and sounded foreign) and don't mention that after they left you dragged yourself (and the chair you were tied to) to the panic button and pressed it with your chin and the security company took forty minutes to come and so you had ample time to think and mostly you thought

Wonderful! I am alive!

Spade

by Katleho Kano Shoro

There are stories and aches you've buried in bottomless silence.
The daughter in me believes you are protecting her from the hearing.
The you in me decides it's your own sanity you're preserving.
If, on any quiet evening, you need to unearth them,
the you in me can help carry them in and out of mourning without
  being seen.

Burials
by Fiona Zerbst

Plague time. Rags and crosses
dot the sand. Nobody wants to
cry above the sound of the now-dry
river, or the sough of wind.

Sand fans out around the morning.
Frail, tea-coloured fingers pick
at blankets. Two hands rub along
the beadwork nubs of spine, a woman

crying at this touch, as touch
is only pain. A dozen losses
knot up, like a weathered rope,
as grief builds in the throat again.

Plague time. Bones and crosses.
Burials. A dead bouquet.
Nobody wants to tell of this, or
hear of this. They want it to go away.

Finsong
> by Isobel Dixon

Alphabet of breath
and fish and fowl,
words the gills and wings
of the world we love and suffer in.

Kingdom of mackerel skies,
the cloud's anatomy,
glottal branches of sense,
beautiful trachea, click-locking vertebrae.

We husband our resources,
tend. O tender emperor,
your cheer a mute command,
more subjects than you dream unwind

the bandages. The curling scrolls,
inscrutable cells. The dorsal fin
of fortune flicks, scales flex.
Mutable, curious, entire,

unfurl in the flux,
the deep, beyond-breath alphabet.

i.m. James Harvey

The first time
  by Colleen Crawford Cousins

At two, in the narrow backyard
I look up
at the blue rectangle of sky
bisected by the clothesline's flapping squares
The sky is very deep.
For the first time, I think:
I am alive!
I am here!
And I know exactly where here is,
between the back door
and the garage wall.

July

by Fiona Zerbst

July. The sodden grass. And leaves that cling,
resisting, to my boots. A solemn cry,
as doves, now settled in a palm tree's dry
enclosure, lose the will to chat or sing.
July. My eyes are sore. This light is wet
yet brassy, even smug, and minutes pass
the way a drop will slide across the glass:
too slowly, blindly. And I can't forget

July. The way it shimmers, glossy, damp,
like hair, or like a field of trodden grass.
I can't forget the things that cannot pass
before the eye, as shadows pass a lamp.
I can't forget the light, these flightless birds,
and all my dull, distraught and useless words.

Winter From A Balcony

by Jenna Mervis

five o clock winter sun on the mountainside breaks
through clouds in zigzag shine between icicle
gums; there's more rain in those grey tenements
overhead, more chilled rasps of air to be inhaled
or fought off with fleece and fake fur; even the eyes
are cold enough to freeze tears, and snot stops short
of nostrils' thresholds crusting like stalactites and mites;
I'm pissing coffee, tea, hot anything from the kettle;
clasped tight to my stomach is a bottle of warmth
and later a man who'll turn in at night with his hot
head and warm blooded panting to heat our sheets;
or an electric blanket you can't marry or cook for
but want to kiss each time you crawl under its skin;
time drags the sun across the sky like a reluctant dog
bucking at the end of its leash not another step further
on its nimbostratospheric chain soaked with rain –
the cumulative effect of afternoons like this one; even
the house shivers and curses, brick by brick, the drizzle.

Telltales

by Margaret Clough

I could tell a storm was coming
by the harshness of the seagull's cry
and the way the dog shivered
as he hid behind the chair
and the sound of the door, banging
and by seeing, lying at the sky's corners,
the fine-drawn strings of cloud
like the frown lines forming
round my eyes.

Miskien / Maybe by Annette Snyckers

Miskien

Op daardie oggend
sal ek opswem
uit slaap
boontoe skop
uit 'n donker droom
na die lig daarbo,
die eerste asem
van die geel dag neem –
en besef:
alles het verander.

Maybe

On that morning
I shall swim up
from sleep
kick upwards
from a dark dream
to the light above,
draw the first breath
of the yellow day –
and realize:
everything has changed.

Saturday: Spreading the news
by Beverly Rycroft

The colour of the grass is green
the colour of the sky is blue
Georgia's hair is blonde
it shines in the sun.

Georgia's father is John
he wears a red shirt
John is walking across the green grass
to tell Granny.

John is the magic man he
wades through the colours and
the colours don't know or even
suspect the words he is smuggling
down their pretty path.

Can you see me?
I'm at the lounge window.
I'm watching John as he
walks down the path and
carries the words
to give Granny.

The grass is green today
the sky is very blue
Georgia's hair is blonde
John's shirt is red
Granny wears a pink dress

The words
are black and white.

Home

by Khadija Tracey Heeger

I have to draw maps.
I have to ride my feet like chariots.
I have to speak like stone and rock.
I have to see like water.
I have to love like mother tongue.
I have to wrestle with the bones of my dead.
I have to wade through the sands, leap through the dungeons
so I feel,
so I feel as I wonder through my life
not knowing me, not knowing now.
See my mirrors and my footprints dance,
me my back to the wind posing in the cracks of my winded smile.
See my questions barren, black shoving marks against these walls,
burning holes in charcoal dreams.
I am here but seldom seen.
I am here,
I am.

I have to draw maps.
I have to ride my feet like chariots.
I have to speak like stone and rock.
I have to see like water.
I have to love like mother tongue.
I have to wrestle with the bones of my dead.
I have to wade through the sands, leap through the dungeons.

so I know,
so I know the dust-stamp footfall,
a murmuring earth call,
knowing where, knowing how
knowing me, knowing now.

I have to draw maps
to make the swindler mute
to sound the horn
to speak by using my own tongue and annihilate the mutant words.
I have to ride my feet like chariots
to win her back
to find her soles and grow my own
in the new places I call home.

I have to wrestle with the bones of my dead
so I may live here in their stead
carrying their wisdom on the lean road
learning the lessons by which I am lead.

I have to wade through the sands,
leap through the dungeons
to find her footprint, to find her footprint
to make a footprint
to make a footprint of my own
so I will know
that I am
home.

The existence of home
by Karin Schimke

And you could never abjure your birthright
though you never went back. What for?
And you could never accept your permanence.

Everything chafed. But it was you all along: rubbing
your own sun-browned skin raw against the hemispheres,
always suspecting the existence of home.

Tong / Tongue by Annette Snyckers

Tong

Ek vou my tong
om my taal, versigtig –
want sy hou haar
soms opsy.
Ek flonker mos flikkers
vir die ander
hulle klanke bekoor my,
hulle woorde verlei.

Ek ontdek ander ekke
in vreemde tale –
saam reis ons
na verre lande,
maar tuis
vou ek weer my tong
om my taal, gemaklik –
sy proe soos my plek.

Tongue

I fold my tongue
around my language, carefully –
because she keeps herself
apart sometimes.
I flirt with the others
their sounds charm me,
their words seduce.

I discover other selves
in strange languages –
together we travel
to far countries,
but at home
I fold my tongue
around my language again, with ease –
she tastes like my place.

in a strange land
    by Marike Beyers

as strange as anyone
looking for a sprig of green

the city rises   rises here
the country of everywhere
ten million feet from platform to platform
at 4 o'clock the windows shut

I see the walls   I hope
I step out   it's not falling

every day is the death of first rain
and flowers   rows and rows
as the guards come on
count the boots the coins
the trains rushing by

if the world had hands
could I have been

the if of life and I hold it in my mouth
the I – I unreturned
a small stone held in the hand
I cannot keep it myself
but who else

Sign Poem 18

by Eliza Kentridge

Dark evening
Aslant in a chair in the dark kitchen
Through windows and skylights
I try to catch the night in the round

Planes blink amid the stars

I make out shapes in the garden
The studio roof
The sputnik barbecue
Trees make diagrams for the planes
They draw on the napkin of the sky
Here's how you get from A to B
North to South
East to West
The pilots check their instruments

STRAIGHT ON TIL MORNING

The undercarriages reflect life on earth
Their shifting lights echo lights on the river
Red and green signals flicker on the flat calm of the water
An unseen channel mapped
Downstream in the darkness
The sea awaits its sons and daughters

One of the planes catches my thought
Takes it on its wishbone

Carries it over European landfill
To make landfall with the African continent
Shaped exactly like itself

PLEASE HAVE YOUR BOARDING CARDS READY

For some time now the geese have been gathering
Hustlers at the water's unravelling edge
A pit stop on their road trip through heaven
Cool dawn wakes us to their flap and call

I READ MUCH OF THE NIGHT AND GO SOUTH IN THE WINTER

Daily, nightly, I tread the boards
The boardwalk, the promenade, the jetty
Looking eastwards
Like Marlow at anchor on the *Nellie*
Light thickening and darkening over Gravesend
Estuary flooding outwards to the sea
The yacht swinging on the tide
Light surging and dimming on the Essex marshes

LOOKING INTO THE HEART OF LIGHT

The darkness
The silence
We share this at any rate
Remembering and misremembering Africa

Words to take to a desert island
  by Colleen Crawford Cousins

I'll take tough handy words:
Axe, knife, rope, bang
And, of course, the basics –
Fern, loam, leaf, loaf
For comfort:
Cool, cavernous, cumulous, pillow
Against loneliness,
Damask, chiton, bandeau, tango
For mental stimulation, I'll pack the puzzling
Promise, soon, and pure
To use as weeks wear on I'll bring
Baleen, billow, sheetrock, ambergris
And a few small luxuries that don't weigh much
(Sidereal, fledgling, helicon, ghee)
Oh, and I'd like to pack the (possibly impractical)
Promiscuity
Always and never (those vertical cliffs of stone)
I'll leave at home.

When I finally get to Bhutan
by Karin Schimke

I will have to eat stars to be guided back.
The Southern Cross on my wrist. I will have to hold
Orion's belt out to him. I will have to know
that the dust I breathe is home dirt just so
that I can carry it all back, carry it all on my back.
I will stand at the bare feet of Gangkhar Puensum
with Venus in my armpit and wind-dogs
at my ankles. I will wait there for a passport
or a transit bus or a bridge or loose roots
and think about the last climb. I will not climb.
I will drink a cup of water while I wait. I will be glad
to go home.

Materiality
   by Isobel Dixon

makeshift   shipshape   deepspace
     early scary dreams
roughsmooth   blackwhite
shapeshift   swellshrink
        mineshaft
        brainshift
     silken silent scream

Dark Matter
does the dark matter
     O, the dark mutters
     Dark Mother
     a darker moth
    the darkling mote –

me-grained
megrimmed
     a mute has-been

Sign Poem 7

by Eliza Kentridge

Here is the dirt road where my days are spent
Drawn margin of the village
Stage and playground for half my life
Quite surprising when you think about it
The surprise of landing up
The surprise of where life spills you and where you hang on

ARCHAEOLOGICAL TIME

A Victorian road running from farm to river
Crossing a railway line running from London to the sea

UP AND DOWN THE CITY ROAD
IN AND OUT THE EAGLE

Marshlands here and the famous wide sky

RESIDENTS PARKING ONLY

Though everyone parks as they please

20 MILES PER HOUR
CHILDREN PLAYING

And so are summer sparrows in hollows full of dust

All this English ease of access to wetlands and the sea
While I come from dry uplands in another hemisphere

In my dreams we are on the koppie
Lizards resting on hot stones
Johannesburg opening out to the north a sea of trees
In the distance the Magaliesberg

TO HELL AND GONE

ON A HIDING TO NOTHING

HALF WAY TO VOETSAK

Here Victorian builders came to work
Moleskin trousers and tiny clay pipes
They dug these earth foundations, handbuilt this terrace
Meat pies and ale at a pub near the shipyard
Johannesburg still a mote in its mother's eye

This row built for ships' captains
A terrace gently hoiking itself up the hill
Sail lofts, fireplaces, sash windows
While there – scrubby veld and ridges of rock
Gold unbothered in the ground
Lizards above, and eagles, a variety of buck
Meerkats
Quite possibly leopards

WHAT POWERS OF RECALL

And then the whole history
A whole city conjured into being
A whole society dug from the earth

AM I RIGHT?

Meanwhile here the village carried on
People wandered up this same road to the farm

SIMULTANEOUS HISTORY

SPONTANEOUS COMBUSTION

A ship built for the Prince of Wales
Railings carted off to make World War guns
The river rising and falling in its tides
Sheep grazing and bleating
Shorebirds tracking the water's edge

WE HAVE BEEN THROWN BACKWARDS

I know dirt roads in the south

The road to Retief's Kloof
Beyond the padlocked gate
The huge boulders we slid down into the rock pool
And the view over beloved Transvaal bush

HOW I MISS THE BUNDU

Orange roads through green Transkei landscapes
Dongas and ruts chopping the surface
Our car's shock absorber bent double
But a man under a tree fixed it
Took it off and bashed it straight on the selfsame tree

RIGHT AS RAIN
HOW CAN WE THANK HIM?

Money of course and memory
The car fine for years after that

YOU'LL NEVER BELIEVE WHAT HAPPENED

It got us down the buckled road to the sea
Tropical fields giving way to a blanket of blue
Great miles of sand laid on for us
Thin boys and their cattle wandering through the foam
A mirage approaching til they passed
Big smiles and waves, huge humpnecked Afrikanders
Horns spreading wide, ribs

Another car story
Remember that time after the game reserve?
Something wrong with the engine
All of us piled out on the roadside like luggage
Various useless attempts at tinkering

WHAT DO LAWYERS KNOW ABOUT ENGINES?

Our family friend lolling on the verge
Novel in hand
Pale American in a hat
The most useless of the lot

OH YE OF LITTLE FAITH

At the appointed time
Known only to himself
He rose
Placed his hands upon the engine
And fie! The bloody thing started

SHYSTERS THE LOT OF THEM

That road down to the river at a Knysna farm
Hanging on in the back of a 4 x 4
Wheels skimming the edge of a ravine
Fragile trees, almost a rainforest, filling the hollow
Imaginably crushable were we to fall
Would they catch us if we fell?

DON'T LOOK
I WANT TO LOOK

The bakkie jolting over boulders and roots
We are side by side with precipitous death
Holding on by our fingertips
The sun burning our noses

NOW THAT'S WHAT I CALL A GOOD ROAD
MY FAVOURITE KIND OF ROAD

With a river at the bottom
Crickets and birds loud in the heat
A wild fig to shade the rugs
Then running over sharp pebbles to the brown shallows
Wafting in layered currents
Cliff jumpers splashing in near a canoe
The scene lapped into camera screens and phones

COME OUT NOW
YOU'RE GETTING BURNED

Hats, sunscreen

YOU'RE ALREADY BURNED

All those years of craziness
Frying up like a full English next to the pool
Lobsterine on the beach
Shoulders peeling in layers like mica
And now the mottled damage
Fearful checking of moles, molehills

BUT THE ENGLISH WOMEN!

What fine and creamy skin
Skin stretched softly over breastbones
Cheeks younger than their years
Necks plump and uncrabbed
Ripe for vampires

I COULD KISS YOU NOW

A rough boy once lay beside the pool
My truanting neighbour
A cigarette for homework
Smoking hot in the heat

A SNAKE CAME TO MY WATER TROUGH

And I, not pyjama'd
But cased in navy tunic and brown socks
Stupid hat stuffed between books
His blatant disregard for rules
My primly ruffled sensibility

I AM AFFRONTED SAID MRS TIGGYWINKLE

NOBODY SHOULD BE ALONE AT THE POOL

Him sizzling rudely in trunks
The pine trees and bougainvillea reflected in blue water
Me speechless at the cheek of him
Me speechless at the sight of him
Or is that the trick of years?

So troubled a boy, it must be said

I DIDN'T KNOW YOU

Motorbikes roaring all night
Racing in the dark down the jacaranda avenue
I wished them dead
Vicious tripwires in my head
And then one died
Turns out he was your friend

I'M SORRY

I had no idea of my own power

The reckless sleeper
by Haidee Kotze

   Time,
I thought.
Coffeed & inked. Light scarred against mirrors while she practised the world
on paper. Kafka crumbling against the comfort of spoons, scarves, skin.
   Time,
I thought.
Desire watercoloured, worn like a locket. Who dares not to speak?
Not to run like a child after a blue pigeon? Not to offer the mouth for eating,
not to follow? Who dares not to? Step in, fall through. Kissing crows and
candles. Again.
   Time,
I thought.
And Leonard wept as she chose the colours of this place:
rhubarb, tea stains, ginger, asphalt, biscuit, scissors, guinness, tongue,
memory, bone, canvas, railway, wax, egg, fire.
   Time,
I thought.
A reckless sleeper. A puzzle of objects, a guarding blanket. The horror of a
blue ribbon. The hollowness of hats. Something to touch.
   Time,
I thought.
Walking through revolving doors.

The Tate Modern/Starbucks, London

Relativity

by Helen Moffett

In a parallel universe, I live
in a small New England college town;
I teach on campus; so does my husband.
We're both scrambling through the rat-pace
of the publish-or-perish tenure-track race;
I have two children and never enough time.
I live in a clapboard house (no picket fence)
with hardwood floors I pad across in socks.
I am familiar with the scrunch of snow underfoot;
own things like ear-muffs; worry about the boiler.
Some things are the same; in the kitchen,
a box for recycling, tub for compost scraps,
a fridge bright with magnets and memorabilia
except here they call it refrigerator.

Am I happy? I think so. My children
have taught me what love is, how it
embeds in soul and flesh. My husband
is kind, clever, handsome in certain lights;
we live past each other mostly,
a fact we bemoan at the occasional
dinner snatched together, before talk
turns to the kids; is the new school
working out? Becky begged for
violin lessons, now won't practice:
should we push her, persevere? But
we still make love on weekend afternoons
when the children are out the house,
shrugging off the slight sensation of
one more thing ticked off the list.

At nights I fall into the embrace
of our sheets, swooning for sleep,
knowing that the next morning
the entire mechanism will be kicking
in relentlessly, ticking frenetically.

I had my chance to make the quantum
leap to this alternate world. In my present one,
I'm just as short of time. I do get to have
great gobs of alone (perhaps too much):
but I know it's the one thing my parallel self
pines for with something akin to homesickness.

Repetition

by Tariro Ndoro

After Sherman Alexie

1. Some things go on forever. 2. The rest keep coming back like a boomerang. 3. The moon moves in cycles, she goes to come back. 4. Sometimes waves are caused by the dancing of the moon, the earth and the sun, we call this a tidal wave. 5. Every decade the rains forget my country, we call this drought. 6. ESAP gave birth to my generation. 7. We suckled acrid milk from mothers who themselves were starving. They called it sacrifice. 8. A decade goes by and the moon, the stars and the sun move. Rain forgets to visit my home again. We call this famine. 9. The moon moves in cycles, she goes to come back. 10. Sometimes waves are caused by the dancing of the moon but these waves in my body give birth to blood. 11. Every moon cycle, the female body cramps in spasms, we call this dysmenorrhoea. 12. Sometimes the uterus bleeds so heavily, it almost kills its host, this is menorrhagia. 13. My generation learnt to speak in the shadow of kwashiorkor. This is a lack of protein. 14. Again, my generation moves towards starvation towards scorched earth towards oblivion. We call this pain... The moon circles round the earth and the earth around the sun like a boomerang and times pulls us back to swallowing heavy names of heavy diseases we could never quite pronounce no less cure.

Recurral

by Beverly Rycroft

Do you lie awake at night,
cousin Nolan wants to know,
and wonder if it will come back?

Like a dog that
once peed on a lamppost?

Yes.
No.

But sometimes I dream
it's 3 a.m. and my doorbell is ringing.

A taxi has been circling my
neighbourhood for years
and finally found

the right address.

Beyond

by Fiona Zerbst

Let me fall asleep. Awake,
I pause before that inner door
and wonder what I listen for,
and how much is at stake.

Let me go to sleep. I take
the route of thorn and lavender,
of thistle, dew and fruitlessness,
of loveless words. I ache

for more than life can offer me.
The little stream, the sanctuary,
are not enough. I hunger for
the dreams that take me, more and more,

beyond that shut, that inner, door
beyond which is a lake.

What mountains dream of
  by Helen Moffett

Slumbering in the sheet of heat
smoothed gently across the Little Karoo.
No wind. Only warmth, but it doesn't press.
It floats, draping the spines and ribs
into which history has folded these ranges.
Raging hormones of the earth's adolescence
blasted entire continents into the sky
leaving the remnants to drift down and lie
locked into peace, immobile, their flanks
not even twitching in the drowsy summer
afternoons. Now they breathe in time with
the slowly passing centuries of geology's clock,
the beat too deep to resonate in our bones.
But the mountains hear it in their sleep:
tick, and then: aeons later, tock.

for Dan and Vindra Reddy

Tide

>by Joan Metelerkamp

Low tide like out breath   wake
with sore neck, stiff back, wrestled all night

like the sea in the dead of night still
out there, talking to itself, continuing, arguing;

the urging sea, the sea urges, breaking itself open urgently
slowly retreats, turns its back: if you don't get up
and do something productive that's your problem –
it's done what it can – it too will lie flat
as if everything were done and said already, already wasted –
again a perfectly boring perfect day what spaces
under your arms as you lie on your back
sea so flat you can see under the waves little crenellations of sand;

just now the wind will lift a little saying the sea
is starting again sucking at its old sources.

At the World's End

by Elisa Galgut

Here, in this harbour city, we've withered in another winter.
The damp is everywhere, the books are mouldy,
Evening lies on the slate-grey sea.

Despite the cold, we leave the windows open
And listen to the roar of pebbles upon the strand.
The sliver moon rising above the mountain

Casts a faint light on the valley below.
We have lived from birth in this fist of rock
And ocean. We have barely seen the sun.

We are the ghost people. We make plans
Each day for the trek across the summit,
But the petals still divert us with their scent

As we wait for the wind to deliver our final spring.

Littoral

by Colleen Crawford Cousins

I am in the place where dreams don't speak
the edge of the sea when the tide is out
the waves recede
the sand shines
the gulls stand in small battalions

the wind has something to say
the wind speaks in riddles

if I'd woken earlier
if I'd come here when the moon still sailed
blinking urgent signals to the night clouds
while the stars kept on winking –

and out to sea, out to sea
past the big bass of the droning waves
I know the South Pole smiles so icy
I'm here, the end, the beginning of this rolling world
trust me when the planet turns

Patterns
by Fiona Zerbst

There is no peace
on earth.

Gravity makes its noise,
a factory hum;

the body's parts protest and shunt,
creak into life,
go on with will and blindness,
working cogs.

This poem
aches and chafes
for the belt to stop;

for lines and threads
to finger a pattern of birds
or flowers
on a rag of silk.

Hadeda geographies
by Melissa Butler

Hadedas are nothing much to notice
until you hear them—*haa haa dee dah*.
Some consider them a nuisance
that interrupts morning love-making
or evening conversations on the veranda,
but for others their call echoes home.
It is often said they call for the rain
or call about it coming. I think
they might be saying something else.

Southern Right Whales come each winter
to breed—swim in playful circles
close to shore. Their large flukes sailing
with the wind, rough white patches
on their heads. People travel great distances
for boat rides and coastal hikes
that bring them closer:
close enough to hear
what these ancient beings have to say.

The dassie is a small rodent-like creature
who lives in mountain rocks and trees
near the sea. It is the closest living relative
to the elephant. I love that someone
figured this out: noticed similarities
between tusks and incisors, studied

pads on soles of feet, traced
the abdominal placement of testes
to a large, distant relative.

Stories seem to evolve with animals:
How leopard got so many spots, why
crocodile has big teeth, the reason
crow sings inside a full moon. But stories
are not only for children. We need them
to tell us what things mean.
So we know what matters
and when to let go.

People migrate to the city each day—
a tide of uniformed blue washing in
with the first glimpse of light
and washing out as the sun casts
deep orange low on the horizon.
The circadian of the city. Every day,
except Sundays, this happens. People come
and go in a rumble of earth—a pulse
that remains after they have moved on.

Hadedas travel almost the same route
every day. They are punctual to and from
their feedings—*haa haa dee dah*.

They are as predictable as morning coffee
or late afternoon tea. Their rhythms
follow the moon. They come and go
underneath a scumbled sky
pushing sea against sea.

Mollusks begin as larvae,
then attach their mantles
to fish hosts for nutrients
that grant them freedom to leave,
to move on to other places: boulders,
fishing boats, whales.
Some of these places travel;
others stand still. I wonder
if mollusks can tell the difference.

Animals get clues to tell them
when to move; they follow sun or stars,
scent, magnetic field, memory. They go
in search of water or food, a better climate.
They go where they go to get what they need.
Some movement is grand: wildebeest
in tides across the Serengeti. Others travel
outside our view: a blanket of moths
in a night sky or a lone sea turtle mother
seeking land to lay her eggs.

Touch sends signals
from the bottom layer of skin
through the spinal cord to the brain.
This path registers the feeling,
tells us where we are,
that there is something to know.

Bees go into and out of petals
to collect what they need.
A metronome of wings in pursuit
of what tastes sweet, what nourishes larvae,
what might become honey.
Some bees go home at night,
but others stay to drift asleep
inside the hold of a flower.

Hadedas fly to the ground
in pairs—*haa haa dee dah*.
They land in cattle kraals and open fields
to probe the earth
with long downward curved bills.
They eat earthworms and insects, spiders
and snails. They feed by what they feel.
They feel to feed.

What begins as mountain or hillside
eventually turns to sand.
Time moves in this way. But dreams
are a different kind of time.
They work in labyrinths
to send glimpses we cannot count.
Dreams open what we hold in our skin:
footsteps, salt, stories.

Galaxies hold solar systems and solar systems
hold stars, planets, asteroids and moons.
There are billions of galaxies layered in this way.
Everything is where it is
because of the push and pull of things
in relation to their mass.
This is all we are:
matter in constant tug with other matter,
trying to hold on to our place.

Some creatures build their homes
out of habit: beavers, ants, spiders, birds.
If something comes along to destroy the place
where they live, to sweep it away or step on it,
if it gets dismantled by weather or human hands,
what happens is this: they build it again;
collect branches or twigs, haul pieces of sand,
find another place to begin.

Male baboons stay with a troop only
for so long before they leave to disperse
themselves in a Southerly,
in search of another place.
Every so often a baboon does not find his way
to a new troop and so he stays alone.
Some people think this is sad,
but it is the way of things.

Hadedas do not perch, but they do come home.
It is here where they nest and do their billing—
intertwine necks and preen each other.
They grasp bills and rattle:
move their heads up and down, side to side.
This is how they ask each other to stay.
This is how they tell each other what matters:
touch, sky, holding on—*haa haa dee dah*.

I want to know how to find my way home.
Not by sight or sound
or following a map. I want to feel it
without my mind tackling it down.
Know it like the hadedas know
when to leave and when to stay.

I want to feel this kind of knowing:
how it threads its way through me, how it
pulls me in, where it shows me to go.
I want to know from a place
outside of what we know about knowing,
away from dream or memory;
somewhere inside instincts of skin.

I want to know what the spiders know,
what the sea turtles tell their young,
what moths want from the wind.
I want to feel movement across fields,
the tug of magnetism against my breath.
I want the urgency of it all: the need to take,
to go, to come back.

I want to hold what cannot be known,
fold it into me, let it stay. And then maybe
I will find what the hadedas have to say:
what they call for, what they want from us,
what they know about knowing
and letting go—*haa haa dee dah*.

To open up words, /
umfold them to paper

What the dead say
  by Phillippa Yaa de Villiers

Cities stand
like ravished women
called Maputo, Accra, Mombasa;
on a beach of bleached
memory.

Torn, shattered, only half-
decent, with that lewd, innocent look around the eyes
that girls get when they've been used too soon:
they know how to please and how to get
what they need. They watch sailors come
and go.

The waves blow the mind
back to the first sharp pain as
hard men forced themselves in
and buildings bled history
into the soil of time. Now a tattered
cover-girl seduces
visitors to exotic destinations while
the dead walk the streets,

their last cries woven into the bricks of its fortresses:
'We have no place in this history they say
is ours. Who are these heroes? Strangers stare
out of books
like products in foreign shop windows. Please,
please show me a picture of me,
tell my story.'

Stories

by Wendy Woodward

We will all die from a lack of stories.
Ishi, the last 'wild Indian'
in California in the 1930s,
cossetted by anthropologists,
died of a cold,
but silence already had him by the throat,
as surely as snaring wire.

The last oyster-catcher
on larval rocks
pit-pits conversations
for feathered ghosts
rehearsing the minutiae of her day:
the squabbling seagull,
the morsel lost to the sea.

The last Knysna elephant
lives with such loss, too.
She speaks to whales
who hear her sonar rumble.
They pass with speed
seldom now
that their world is deafened.
They tell of lost precision,
of depth soundings
adrift in darkening seas.

The silence subsides,
a little, for the old elephant,
at such encounters.
Her stories creak into mobility,
but comfort never accompanies her
as she returns, solitary again,
to blend with the boulders,
solid like beloved companions,
yet irrevocably speechless.

Foolish mermaid
    by Crystal Warren

for the sake of a man
I forsake the safety of the sea

cut out my tongue
walk on glass

dance for your smiles
the words you will not say

slowly I fade away –
foam upon the shore

Bertha Mason Speaks
by Michelle McGrane

Now that you've heard Jane's side of the story, what I wish to tell
you is this:

that once I had hoped to be happy with my cold, dour-faced
husband somewhere in the periphery; that, in retrospect, the day
he came for me was the day my island spirit deserted me; that the
exile from my ramshackle green home caused something within
me to tear adrift;

that I dreamed of sticky-sweet mango strings caught between
my teeth, awaking with a salty mosaic tattooed on my lips; that
I basked naked in the arms of a calypso moon with seashells
gleaming in my untamed mane; that all of the bonnets and
baubles in Christendom could not compare to the sunshine of
Spanish Town;

that I floated on a celestial conflagration of saffron frangipani
only to plummet, petrified, into a voodoo tomb; that within these
stone walls time became obsolete: no market days, no festivals, no
seasonal ebb and flow; that mocking echoes dogged this stifling
boudoir and rattled within my bones;

that while I stalked the corridors of the haunted mausoleum,
cinders and sparks showered their benedictions upon me; that
I invoked the shapes of incandescent fever-trees, both eclipsed
candle and hungry flame; that I sang, blood-red, the island's
setting sun, despite my dislocated tongue.

The Minotaur comes to our picnic
by Wendy Woodward

Give me a glow-worm, not Ariadne and her silly string,
a being of tunnels who is his own light.
He will guide me to the Minotaur
simmering at the end of the labyrinth.
Settling on the ceiling, he'll offer a silhouette
in this subterranean cave of the one who slowly murders
the heroes who trundle up the path to his lair.

How the beast smiles at their jingling footsteps,
swords reflecting the gleams of their little lights,
soon to be snuffed out.

Coming into the day could be deadly
for this heavy hybrid,
for he lacks experience of openness,
yet he commits to it, trotting fatly down bone-littered corridors.
Knights in armour flatten themselves as we pass,
but I have him by the nose as he steams,
sulphurously, towards the sunlight.

Once on the surface, we fear him less,
decorate the curls on his forehead with lilacs.
He plays a little, in the fynbos, delighting in our company
but tires, soon, of the exercise, his eyes wincing at the light.

When he snores, we consider piercing his hapless heart,
but we need him below, fulminating in the darkness,
testing the bravery of our smug suitors.

We feed him pine nuts and cherries
when he wakes and show him the entrance of his tunnel

which he staggers into, tripping drowsily
on glistening hooves.

He smiles at the edge of the darkness,
promising return, with a tally of his conquests
chalked mnemonically, for our benefit,
on granite walls.

Envy

by Phillippa Yaa de Villiers

I envy women
with the clean envelope
of their pleated sex
unwritten on.
No acrid spill of ink to
interrupt the smooth serenity
of their being, flowing without interference
into the eternity of their imagination.
Behind their curtain of conformity
they spin their continuity,
embroider their stories
on walls of crisp linen,
weave blankets of homilies,
comforted by repetition.
Safe.
This is their time:
they will step on to the stage of this
enamoured century, like
a missing actor coming to take her place.
Her big night is here.
We, the incoherent
watch from the wings.

Faith

by Margaret Clough

Not the stained glass window warrior
sword in hand,
nor the sea captain, steadfast through the storm,
but warmth spreading slowly under thick blankets,
and in the darkness
remembering the feel
of a small hand closing round my finger.
Outside my window
a sudden owl swoops then flies back
to make a quiet moaning in the pines.
I hear the rustle of birds.
Dawn coming.
I am aware of wings.

the end
    by Haidee Kotze

apocalypse is the first thing after   after
a landslide of red   dreams of black crêpe &   broken glass
a lifetime of nuclear waiting to happen

today i hide while the sky melts like rubber   like a guy fawkes ode
with tomorrow cross-stitched between my legs   sap dripping into my shoes
how else to bleach out afternoons of petrol   strychnine &   rapists on hot tar

always a taste for tightness you had &
me shopping for boys who push my panic buttons
who thought who   thought this

finally after   after
years of keeping still to escape
the horseman and his choir of maggots pining for blood

the maid of orleans does a slow minuet
for the unwilling dead

How the architect lives
by Karin Schimke

At night alone in a tower
he draws the boxes
that will become rooms.
He shoots a digital diagonal
into space previously occupied
only by itself. He tilts a world
towards the sun to move the light,
and breaks horizons into heartbeats.
He unfurls fire escapes and draws lifts
up imaginary shafts. He raises roofs beyond
the call of geometry. He whispers at unbuilt corners
to coax a pulse into the veins hidden inside walls.

Late. Late. Outside the window now
is a crashed constellation. He opens his palm
and blows on it till a small city pops up. He
doesn't think of clocks while he measures
the make-believe bathrooms and kitchens,
imagined here in this calculus of planning.

Soon it will be done. Until then, he
works parallel to the ancient light,
dreaming it undreamt.

art

by Thandi Sliepen

matted hair a
yellow felt cap
like a half moon
shading my mind
just looking to survive
unstable ground i
snag in overgrown gardens
though the mornings are
full of birds swimming
inside my ears

Not every piece

by Joan Metelerkamp

Not every piece has to be the whole story
not every day

but to keep at the odd row as if it could all grow
one day into a field full of cabbages

or more like a plain
cardigan for a granddaughter;

there's only so much looking down and sticking
to your knitting you can do;

only so much sitting in the kitchen.
But I do like the kitchen floor –

why not look at its uneven tiles
the bottom of a rock pool recalled
down at the wild side –

and the table's legs shaped
like the legs of a slender bushbuck
let them stand for a day.

To Christina Rossetti

by Helen Moffett

Those years, sitting in the binding hush
of the Bodleian Library,
parchment leaves sifting down outside,
I turned the pages of your tiny notebooks
tracing the progress of each poem;
after the initial burst, words cascading down,
the hard work beginning:
stoking the refining fire,
scouring every line.
I had no idea that one day
I would also wrestle, endlessly
pick at a knot of words, strain to make
language go where I wanted.

I scrutinised your laundry lists,
your letters, even the dull ones of thanks;
at Princeton, in a room glossy with wealth,
they let me hold your hair in my hand.

Perhaps some germ jumped; perhaps
I learnt more than I knew;
perhaps you showed me
that poetry is possible; a strange fuse
of voices in the head and hands braced for toil.

Waiting for Harry
by Crystal Warren

once there was a boy
who became a wizard
with magic so strong
when he cast his spell
a world was enchanted

Imagination

by Sindiwe Magona

Imagination is all the worlds that inhabit you
The worlds that have swallowed you
Since long before you were born.
The worlds all the mothers
And fathers of your race remember
That they have handed down through
The blood in your veins. It is the fire
That burns and scorches all; the ice
That freezes the very breath and leaves
All still. All – all still, deep in your core.
It is the thunder, the lightning, the hail,
And the tranquil song of a grain of sand.
It is the loud bang that shook,
And ceaselessly shakes, the world.
Timeless. Boundless. Beyond
All you can conceive;
Greater than the sum of
Your highest hopes.

The Police Constable/Poet in Court

by Margaret Clough

(Written after I met a constable who liked to write poetry)

Tell us where you saw the accused.
At a place where two roads meet, I stood
and pondered on what path my life would take.
Where exactly were you standing?
At the corner, your honour, of Beach road and Main Street.
And when was this?
The sun had long-since dropped behind the mountain peak
and the moon was painting a silver path across the bay.
What time exactly?
Seven forty five, your honour.
What was the accused doing?
His fingers, stretched like chicken's claws,
clutched at the concrete rim, while his scant and spidery legs,
see-sawed, and scrabbled on the smooth cement.
I beg your pardon?
He was climbing over a wall, your honour.
What did he look like?
All sinisterly draped, dark as night, with features hid in black,
concealing, fleece.
Could you repeat that?
Sorry, your honour, I meant to say he was wearing a black
tracksuit and a balaclava.
And what did you do then?
I called upon the miscreant to render to me an account.
What?
I said "You're under arrest," and hand cuffed him.

The Small Rain
   by Wendy Woodward

Westron wynde, when wylle thou blow,
   The small rayne down can rayne?
Cryst, yf my love were in my armys
   And I in my bed a gayne!
(anonymous 15th-century lyric)

You could rule a line
with the confident rain
on Noordhoek Beach,
falling, battleship grey,
large rain that comes with menace,
dull in its lack of poetry,
over the horizon-sea.

Give me the small rain
of the anonymous poet
who speaks of longing for
her beloved, their union
endlessly deferred
by the prevailing wind,
blowing gently over
the years
into my modern,
empathetic heart.

Lucky Bean Necklace
by Sarah Frost

To write: wear scarlet
seeds threaded through centres black,
girl, stick out your neck

Enough
by Azila Talit Reisenberger

Enough I said.
Enough rearing,
enough raising,
enough kissing,
enough soothing,
enough serving.

Enough I said.
Enough cooking,
enough washing,
enough bill paying,
enough home-making,
enough message taking,
and doctor's room waiting.

Enough I said.
I must conceive again.
Conceive myself.
Write.

Translated by Immanuel Suttner

Words
  by Makhosazana Xaba

Whenever I take the pulse
of my existence
feel the pinch
of my persistence
against the grinding grain
of my resistance
to the pounding punch
of their insistence,
words transmit to me
a drumroll of deliverance.

Rituals

by Crystal Warren

I use words
to counter chaos.

I map the mountains,
exploring peaks and valleys,
avoiding avalanches.

I tell myself stories,
leaving pebbles on the path
so I can find my way home,
one word at a time.

It is a risk
   by Ingrid Andersen

It is a risk
to open up words,
unfold them to paper.

Found vowels,
hidden sibilants
chosen plosives

change shape
on a page.

Statement

by Sindiwe Magona

I come to writing with no great learning
Except my life and the lives of the people
Of whom I am a part. For centuries,
Others have written about us
I write to change that
Instead of moaning about it.
I write so that children who look like me
In my country,
And my people, dispersed
Throughout the world,
May see someone who looks like them
Do this thing that has for so long
Not belonged to us.
I write so that the tale of the hunt
May be heard also, from the mouth of
The hunted; the hated of this world
For only then, will that story
Be anywhere near complete...

Stone words

by Khadija Tracey Heeger

These are my stones,
hard and thankless baggage bending even the strongest spine.
These are my stones,
they have names like anger, fear, hatred, kill, abuse, alcoholic, suicide.
These are my stones,
they go by other names too:
forgiveness, faith, trust, love, friendship, compassion, respect.
These are my stones,
I have chosen them with care.

So hard are my teachers that they lay their hands on me soft as
                                                    God's fingers.
So hard are my teachers that they turn me over and over
till I learn the things I do not want to.
So hard are my teachers that they bend me till I let go into myself
                                              and find God there.

These are my stones and we rub against each other
till my blood paints words on them
and my words paint memory on them.
These are my stones,
they weep, they speak, they live, they laugh
and they love me
till I do.

cradle
    by Haidee Kotze

so far
i have thrown
words like
       wineglasses
           stones
                handgrenades
at the head
of god

but today
i will
go out
to collect some instead –
       soft and round like
       churchbells
           pistachio green
               slippery like
               fresh eggs
                   filled
                   with sap

i will offer them
to you
as a cradle
to sleep in

Ek kan oek mooi woorde skryf
by Shirmoney Rhode

Ek kan oek mooi skryf.
Al sê ek dit skief en krom,
en al is'it nou nie juis geclassify
as deel van die kanon nie,
kan ek oek mooi woorde skryf.

Kanon: die mooiste, mees estetiese.

Ek kan oek mooi woorde skryf.
Soes as ek skryf van'ie roesbruin
flêtse en die krake in die hakke
van die kaalvoete van Mietjie
en my ouma se verimpelde bruin hande
wat'ie meer wil vat soes eers'ie.

Ek kan oek mooi skryf.
Van die afgebriekte hakkiesdraad
en vuil vaal klippies
wat altyd op die veldjie lê.

Ek kan oek mooi skryf.

Fok die kanon.

The Accuracy of Letters
by Elisa Galgut

"The accuracy of accurate letters
is an accuracy with respect
to the structure of reality."*
And so she feels beholden to the words
that shape the world, that represent it,
faithful to the art of living, the craft of writing.
Somehow, the letters must be both transparent
and opaque – allowing the sunlight to filter through,
all the while remaining visible, their characters
sketched in dark font across the endless page.
And in them, through them, is held, in tenuous
balance, the world, both inner and outer,
curled alongside one another like two clasped hands.
The order of thought is the order of things.
As she writes at the close of day, the letters,
like the light, darken; the waning moon appearing
bright and alive above the mountain,
can be written about. Her mind becomes moon-filled.
It glows with light reflected from a dying sun,
which sets below the contours of the page.
Darkness soon will smudge the boundary
between idea and object, between mind and world,
and meaning will be absorbed into the blotting paper of night,
as the letters fall drowsily into shapeless sleep.

* Wallace Stevens, from "The Academic Pieces" in *The Necessary
   Angel: Essays on Reality and the Imagination*

Writer

   by Haidee Kotze

I keep my tools
hidden,
until the sun rasps
its black breath over
the suburbs. Only then

do I edge from
my demure murmuring disguise,
carrying my pen like
an axe,
waiting in the underbrush for
the first bloodwarm faces
to appear. I like

to slaughter the meat out
of them, to space
their soft stomachs across
the page, to stretch
their sinews into
stems and curves,

or else
to pull their wet skins tight,
nailing them down around
the white silences
squirming. I never

wash my hands
after – the whimpers dry
to innocent ink under
my nails. And besides,

I keep my tools
hidden.

The Recalcitrant Muse
   by Michelle McGrane

Sunlight blisters through moth-eaten curtains.
In her mildewed apartment high above the city,
the Muse stumbles out of bed, stubs her toe
in the kitchen as she fumbles for a cigarette,
reheats last night's coffee and loneliness,
gulps it down dark, bitter, thick with grounds
that refuse to dissolve her tongue's furred lining.

She is late for the morning's first appointment
with a middle-aged divorcée at 52 East Avenue.
It's not all it's cracked up to be, this muse business.
She's tired of being aloof, untouchable.
Give me strong hands, warm flesh, a hairy chest,
a plunging prick, fucking on the formica table
She could use a drink. A few hours' sleep.
Immortality doesn't pay the bills.

Muse

by Phillippa Yaa de Villiers

I said to my muse: you never do anything around this place.
She was lying in bed reading poetry. I said
other muses carry water from over two kilometres away.

She asked me to make her a cup of tea.
From the kitchen I shouted: Do you want a biscuit with that?
She said no. She's not greedy or excessive and she tells me

at least twice a day that she loves me. But I can't help feeling
that she's taking advantage somehow.
It's hard to get good help these days.

In the middle of the night
I find her pacing the house
and I say to her, why don't you come back to bed

and she says: shhh..... can't you hear the leaves making love
the heavy heartbeat of the buildings?
There's a crane with its fingers in the mountain's purse...

And I pause
but all I can hear is her breathing
and all I can see is the city surging

surprised
in the reflection
of her headlamp eyes.

Writer's Block

by Jeannie Wallace McKeown

I have writer's block
I have writer's block
I have writer's block

I'm sitting in a coffee shop.
I got the table with the comfy sofa.
My coffee is hot because the waiter
brought me hot milk, even though
I asked for cold.
I'm on holiday and I didn't feel like arguing
on the first day of my holiday.
So I poured in the hot milk.
The coffee is bitter.
One spoon of sugar has made no difference.
I can taste the sugar layered over the bitterness,
but it is still there.
I revel in it.
I have a headache.
The coffee is bitter like medicine.

I have writer's block
I have writer's block

There are blonde women here.
These women are glamorous.

I am in a corner
at the table with the comfy sofa,
sipping coffee with one sugar
and my writer's block
and my belly which shows when I lean back,
and my hair which is silvering.
While I sip my bitter coffee
my ex-husband is driving our children
and his parents
along the coastal road on a journey towards me
in this little town.

I have writer's block
I have writer's block

Nothing has happened yet to write about.
Everything is on a knife's edge of nothing happening,
while he drives along the coastal road
and I wait and sip
and wait.
The coffee shop sells crafts and arts.
Kitsch but I like them.
Beside the sofa four mannequin legs
stretch flatfooted, toes at my earlobe,
plastered and painted in printed paper,
all in the blues.
The radio plays music from the 60s.

Many people have sat on this sofa before me.
My arse slots into the dip they have left.
My arse.
My comfortable arse
with writer's block
while I sip bitter coffee.
My belly trembles so I suck it in.
The blondes have no bellies
and no arses, but
people with arses
have sat on this sofa before,
left their mark.

The waiter tries to take my plate.
I am staring out the window, fork in my hand.
I have eater's block.
This is unusual (see belly, see arse).
My eyes are not seeing the blown tree
or the Coca Cola umbrellas outside.
They are watching the sea on the left
of the car, the traffic on the road,
the wind turbines under which my ex-husband
is driving, with our children and his parents.
I reclaim my plate.
How much easier to resolver eater's block
than writer's block.

I have writer's block
I have writer's block

His parents and my parents have not been together
in four years,
since we split.
This visit is a big deal.
He is bringing them down the coastal road
to my parents' house.
I am not a young woman.
I am not glamorous.
I am not blonde.
My belly shows when I lean back.
My hair is silvering.
I sip bitter coffee on a knife edge in a coffee shop.

Four years since our parents were together.
"You're so lucky," says Jane
(all the artwork is signed *Jane*. Her eyes
are the cobalt blue of the sea.)

 "Divorcing and losing family is hard
but you've kept that friendship."
"Yes, yes, we've worked at it,"
I tell her.

I close my eyes, picture the road,
put myself in the car.

"We've worked hard at it,"
I tell my ex-husband at the wheel.
He turns and smiles,
"We'll be there soon."

I drain the last of my coffee.
I embrace my writer's block,
and my bacon and scrambled eggs.
The blondes have all left.
Two women hold hands over the other table
with comfy sofas.
My ex-husband is driving our children
and his parents down the coastal road.
I am right here;
in the dip in the sofa,
belly and silver hair,
sipping bitter coffee.

Conduit
by Sarah Frost

For how long now
it has been blocked.
The tunnel full of ragged plastic bags, dead branches
washed down from the townships.
The water tainted with faeces.

Stagnant as oil sludge
it pools, dirty, like unresolved pain.

The concrete pipe
fires half-hearted salvoes
into the sea,
a rifle unable to master the waves
muddying its shallow mouth.

Years ago,
a girl walked there with her mother
speaking of who she might become.

Now a woman walks alone
wondering, in the shadows

how she will ever know
what it is she needs to say.

Poisoned water pisses out of the conduit,
fanning the sand beneath it
into delicate patterns.

She holds a glass shard,
smoothed by the sea.

Stands indeterminate
at the edge of the water,
waiting for the clear words to come.

voice
by Marike Beyers

it slips down your throat
    making home inside your chest
you cannot cough it up

it rushes from you
    when you reach for it
you can only wait

you get up one day
    and find this rock on it
your breath seeps out

you cannot move it
    or step around it
you do not know the weight

Taped beak
　　by Karin Schimke

seven songs of self-censorship

i.
seven songs
five and two
for the voiceless
listen now:

　　　　seven
　　　　songs
　　　　seven
　　　　strong
　　　　times
　　　　like
　　　　doh
　　　　ray
　　　　me
　　　　fa

oh there's nil
this song's
chords chime
me wrong
i'm tuning
all along
broken
staves

ii.
write what you know
i only know words
i know only nothing

iii.
over and over
christ this chorus bores me
i'm doing whatever the verb
is for litany and grass grows
over my feet   i am that woman
that white that wash that

i am my own thick black
censor lines my hushing
terrorist up-shutter

iv.
if there are no seeds in the pod
and no water in the bath
and no hope in the apple
if the notes are flat
and i clap ham-fisted
if i am mediocre
and count not a single
original thought
in the lines on my palm
and lack the courage of the sun

to rage on and on
why do i want to burn
paper under the whitewash of ink

v.
i dreamt my cover was blown
soon everyone would know
that i was young, gay, black -
and a man
my alter ego's twitter handle
was @hilaryvent

i taped her beak shut
now her eyes bulge

vi.
all i remember these days
is the tune of forgetting
the ghostly notation
between fading staves
where volume pitch and tone
have narrowed to the
ennui of a middle-c hum
but it's a start

vii.
the start
is the hardest part
and your breath

will catch you out
will catch you
your breath
could close you
your voice could
cloud into the
spaces between
your tongue and
the idea you had of
god

so don't start with god
that's the hardest part
begin with middle c
invoke god from
what's in-between

      (and what is it
      if it is not avarice
      to expect holiness
      from letters and notes
      and what is it
      if it is not greed
      to want more
      than one striving plea).

Points on poems
by Joan Metelerkamp

1. You can begin at any point.

2. You might be asked to account for yourself
    (you are always asking yourself to account for yourself);
    you could start with the point that poems don't sell
    take stock of that fact
    prevaricate, equivocate,

3. leave it as a starting point, for later, balance
    interest, currency, the market;

4. you could come back to it before you had begun you could cycle round
    lugubriously, alternatively

5. get on your bike and ride like hell like we used to, my brothers and I,
    when we were kids –
    careening round the concave concrete cow-shed yard –
    no brakes, no gears –
    sweaty and queasy and
    sometimes skidding on bull-shit.

6. Go, go with its elliptical spin, which is also weirdly comforting because

7. a poem has no point.

8. You could begin again: there is not one point to a poem
    it is always
    another point of departure.

9. Try another point of departure,
      say: poems are like music, not music, but like – the lines
          climax, silence, sound
          their own melodies, yes, but visions
          a score of complex
          moments in process emotion almost beyond words most of all
      what you can hardly, hardly, say, hardly, hardly bear to see, see and then

10. revision. Re-vision, if you must.

11. (Now you see it now you don't).

12. Okay, okay *no ideas but in things* the thing is

13. always the poem:

14. not a record –
      a resonance.

15. But at what point do I come in, you could say,
      and I could say
      either through your eye, through your ear,
      or – what my mother used to say (to thin air)
      when someone in another car hadn't thanked her for letting them in –

16. "not at all".
      Either you get it or you don't.

17. You could ask who speaks when the speaker is I.

18. The point is whose voice, out of the blue, into thin air,
    uses "I", like a child shrieking "me me me",
    or otherwise playing quietly outside under the pines
    whispering "you" "he" "she"?

19. Yours. Mine.

20. The point is: a poem is not a confession,
    it's not a profession (you could go back to the starting point)
    why you do it – it's a puzzle –

21. you could start at the edges
        or go for the gold in the middle –
        the bits where you can't tell
    the reflection from the craft
    floating on the surface, a coracle,
    and the more you piece together
    the figure – like the Lady of Shallot
    drifting through the reeds alone –
    the more she looks like your daughter
    or you, when you were younger,
    only where is the river running you begin to wonder
    and anyway
    there's always a bit missing
    and we all know it doesn't really help –
    the picture, on the box –

22. you're always figuring out
    what isn't fixed even if you think it is: or
    it is
    but still, and precisely still –

23. even though my brother, when we were older
    (though, according to the song, I'm so much younger than that now)
    and I was already a mother,
    used to say: don't fix it unless it's broken.

24. This is an old story
    like Keats's figures on the jar,
    still   chasing
    what they want, what they want to become,
    happy, happy –

    but everything empty, the vessel, the town –
    they'll never be more than they are.

25. A poem is like
    live   drawing   the essential   figure   moving,
    how do you get it moving

26. across the page?
    (There should be no limit to the number of pages.)

27. It has nothing to do with linear narrative
    even though it's made of lines,
    and although it is really a story,

28. where to begin? What is the point
    of entry?

29. The song of the fertility doll (phallic and female)
    the energy that's divine
    (golden girl playing the piano
    easy, jazzy, smiling, explaining
    her hands are two Russian dolls
    they do exactly what she tells them to).

30. What on earth am I talking about – *cling, cohere, persevere?*

31. Don't ask unless you think it's somehow answerable or unavoidable,

32. like voices.

33. St Joan believed even when she couldn't hear the voices any longer

34. to the point of burning alive.

35. What do the voices say?
        What do you feel?
        Can you make them come

36. like someone else's voice? Another poet's?
    These poems are usually the best.
    As though someone else's words came into your head when you wake
    like after the recurring dream of intruders,

you're sweating that fear of death sweat   you've spent all this time
worrying at that point   you know
Eliot made sixty years ago   "the still point of the turning world"

37. and he was only re-writing the ancients and

38. who gives you the right to write what you like
     any way, who's to say if it makes any sense,
     any one – anyway –
     all poems are illegitimate.

39. Get used to this. You can't do anything else.
     Language itself is the transgressor.
     We know this. This is as old as Prometheus.
     "Yes, but what does this mean?"
     Nothing to do with what those who know better call
     "your personal life".

40. Who do you think you're talking to in that tone of voice
     like "get a life"?

41. You, me; myself – a poet is always talking to herself –
     even more than to the dead. Answering back.

42. If the poem makes its own meaning, makes it up as it goes along,
     (I could come back to this) is something (what thing –
     the thing the poem is) prior to the poem –
     need   the question   arise?

43. It does
    arise
    like a god rises
    you can't not
    feel this
    through the slit through the curtains
    white light of the night
    turning to day
    like a lover   turning   over
    through that opening, that parting,
    that deep coming leaving
    only your need
    to speak –

44. Then instead of moving
    through the cool passages of an imagined labyrinth,
    you get your head tangled, line after line
    like a spider in a spider's web:
    Arachne, still weaving the stuff out of herself,
    battered over the head with her own distaff
    by the jealous goddess;
    rather be Ariadne,
    lending her golden thread
    to her hero, to find his way out of the labyrinth,
    yes, he abandons her, but who finds her in the end:
    the one who comes back: Dionysus.

45. What labyrinth?
    When the crystals are dislodged
    the diamond body falls,
    you feel as though you might fall over yourself
    every time you reach upwards,
    even if it's to hang out the washing.
    If you think I'm talking about the inner ear I am.

46. If you are too sentimental or conventional for your crystals
    ever to be knocked out of place
    the poems you prefer will be sentimental and conventional –
    probably in tight little rooms
    (room = stanza, in Italian, no doubt someone will explain)
    with a witty bit left hanging which could be anyone's
    do not disturb sign
    (you never know what's going on in there)
    [of course there are little rooms where when
    is a jar not a jar but a door left just off its jamb
    opening   something we didn't know we could imagine].

47. If you lose your balance completely no one will want to follow
    there.

48. "Sixth and lastly" – as the dogsbody policeman says –
    Much Ado about Nothing –
    the main point about poetry

49. you don't find it in airports or bookclubs,
    and if Nadine Gordimer were to ask you
    if she could publish your work
    for some cause, like AIDS, or even with no cause
    with no payment to you at all you'd say, here, have it *all*,
    please.

50. Cold comfort: the so-called
    helpers at the bookshop in Plettenberg Bay
    have never heard of Nadine Gordimer.
    So how do you make a living, poet, I ask myself,
    not for nothing

51. there are more ways of silencing a poet than with a Sentence.

52. This has nothing to do with The People's Poet.

53. This has nothing to do with The Woman Poet.

54. (The point is, nice girls always lie –
    to protect the innocent –
    there is a point beyond which
    they do not think;
    think what their good friends
    might think.)

55. If it's only amusement play, play,
    taking yourself seriously, amusing yourself, seriously,

see what keeps
coming up
like say you keep coming up with an old symbol,
the Dionysian heart in a basket,
how do you say it –

56. the heart's thought, what does it mean, the eternal return,
    like the baby's heart on the monitor
    your own arrhythmia
    heart in your head on the bed –

    Not the apotheosis but the pattern the poet said.

57. But the pattern always appears
    when you're doing something else
    following some other thread
    you aren't listening or looking
    you're driving towards
    something else,
    like driving in the heat of the day up Keyter's Nek
    to fetch your teenage son after school
    head cruising any way
    into the road's rhythm, the heat,
    windows wide, words gone any way
    like *affirmation of the affirmation*,
    and you know this has very little to do with "positive thinking"
    in fact you're beginning to think it's the opposite,
    the words return, and there's no way to pull off the road,

pull out of its rhythm to look, listen,
to make them some pattern
some sound to hear clearly not like like, like love, like love,
not like this, this,
but I've lost it again like this –
not some thing like love not like any thing but this.

58. Or you wake in the night to the hot still after a storm,
    one of the two black south-eastern warning storms of the season,
    mud smell of water receding,
    frogs down below in the vlei,
    listen,
    an old propeller, an old engine, an old crock car,
    and you don't mind any more where you're spinning in any old world
    nor that the song the frogs make
    makes no more sense than this –
    the ballad the wind sings through the reeds
    through the house on a hot afternoon, sad,
    repetitive, like to a baby in the bulrushes (the heart in a basket)
    the scales you can hear clearly
    of what the poet calls *marvellous*

    out of sight out of mind
    below surface,
    (like a mole-rat shaking and shaking the roots of a khakibos
    and all you can see is the thin plant shaking: okay, take it,
                                        it's just a weed).

59. Below surface, the words of the dead,
    dreams, too.
    I'll make one point: a poet can't live in daylight too long:
    the chainsaw in the valley;
    the chainsong of canaries, cisticolas, sombre bulbul, sunbirds,
    despite the cloud cover;
    the script of named fynbos; the clear horizon, the still sea;
    the discomfort of day's plans, narratives, narratives.

60. Wake to a snippet of dream recalled:
    I am off to get my own handcuffs, my own truncheon,
    hurry up they're waiting for me
    on the other side of the street like opposite the parking lot
    they blew up in Pretoria
    and I am young again as I was then when I lived in Pretoria.

61. Not what he *said* in the dream,
    what he *felt*, felt what I
    felt, I was dreaming, I felt his coming in,
    I think he said something,
    I felt I was coming in like through a door
    through my body
    I felt his cock I took it held it to my breathing
    I am alive so loudly I am grunting in, I am
    aware even in the dream of my breathing
    his speaking saying
    take it
    take it in.

62. I suppose I may have invented him; I may have been given him:
I didn't choose the metaphor, it chose me, came to me;
like a voice, like given words,
a message, open at this passage:
the activity of perception or sensation in Greek is aesthesis which means at root
'taking in' and 'breathing in' – a 'gasp', that primary aesthetic response.

63. Only it didn't feel like a message, but a man.
Like a poem. Not like love but love.

64. There is only one point – begin again – make a poem of it –

List of Modjaji poetry collections

Ingrid Andersen: *Piece Work: Poems* (2010)
Marike Beyers: *How to Open the Door* (2016)
Melissa Butler: *Removing* (2010)
Margaret Clough: *At Least the Duck Survived* (2011)
Margaret Clough: *The Last to Leave: Poems* (2014)
Christine Coates: *Homegrown: Poems* (2014)
Colleen Crawford Cousins: *Unlikely* (2016)
Phillippa Yaa de Villiers: *The Everyday Wife* (2010)
Phillippa Yaa de Villiers: *Ice cream Headache In My Bone: Poems* (2017)
Isobel Dixon: *Bearings* (2016) South African edition published with
    permission of Nine Arches Press in the UK.
Sarah Frost: *Conduit* (2011)
Elisa Galgut: *The attribute of poetry* (2015)
Dawn Garisch: *Difficult Gifts: Poems* (2011)
Megan Hall: *Fourth Child: Poems* (2007)
Kerry Hammerton: *Secret Keeper* (2018)
Kerry Hammerton: *These are the Lies I Told You* (2010)
Khadija Tracey Heeger: *Beyond the Delivery Room* (2013)
Colleen Higgs: *Halfborn Woman* (2004) Hands-On Books
Colleen Higgs: *Lava Lamp Poems* (2011) Hands-On Books
Eliza Kentridge: *Signs for an Exhibition: Poems* (2015)
Haidee Kruger: *The Reckless Sleeper* (2012) Haidee Kruger has since
    changed her surname to Kotze.
Sindiwe Magona: *Please, Take Photographs* (2009)
Michelle McGrane: *The Suitable Girl* (2011) South African edition
    published with permission from Pindrop Press in the UK.
Jenna Mervis: *Woman Unfolding* (2011)
Joan Metelerkamp: *Burnt Offering* (2009)
Joan Metelerkamp: *Making Way: Poems* (2019)

Joan Metelerkamp: *Now the World Takes These Breaths* (2014)

Helen Moffett: *Strange Fruit: Poems* (2009)

Malika Ndlovu: *Invisible Earthquake: A Woman's Journal through Still Birth* (2009) This title is a multi-genre one, and includes poetry, journal entries, essays and resource information.

Tariro Ndoro: *Agringada: Like a Gringa, Like a Foreigner* (2019)

Azila Talit Reisenberger: *Life in Translation* (2008)

Shirmoney Rhode: *Nomme 20 Delphi Straat* (2016)

Beverly Rycroft: *Missing: poems* (2010) Re-published by Dryad Press, 2019.

Arja Salafranca: *Beyond Touch* (2015) Co-published with Dye Hard Press.

Karin Schimke: *Bare & Breaking: Poems* (2012)

Karin Schimke: *Navigate: Poems* (2017)

Katleho Kano Shoro: *Serurubele: Poems* (2017)

Thandi Sliepen: *The Turtle Dove Told Me* (2013)

Annette Snyckers: *Remnants Restante Reste* (2018)

Jeannie Wallace McKeown: *Fall Awake* (2020)

Crystal Warren: *Predictive Text* (2019)

Robin Winckel-Mellish: *A Lioness at My Heels* (2011) Hands-On Books

Robin Winckel-Mellish: *Messages from the Bees: New Poems* (2017)

Wendy Woodward: *A Saving Bannister: Poems* (2015)

Makhosazana Xaba: *These Hands* (2017) First published by Timbila Poetry Project, 2005.

Fiona Zerbst: *Oleander* (2009)

Hands-On Books was started in 2004, and the first title published was Colleen Higgs's *Halfborn Woman*. After Modjaji Books was started in 2007, Hands-On Books became an imprint of Modjaji Books.

Author Index

Printed in the United States
By Bookmasters